Microsoft SQL Server Database Design and Optimization

Lab Manual

WILEY

EXECUTIVE EDITOR	John Kane
EDITORIAL PROGRAM ASSISTANT	Jennifer Lartz
DIRECTOR OF SALES	Mitchell Beaton
DIRECTOR OF MARKETING	Chris Ruel
SENIOR PRODUCTION AND MANUFACTURING MANAGER	Micheline Frederick
PRODUCTION EDITOR	Kerry Weinstein

ISBN 978-0-470-18366-3

Printed in the United States of America

10 9 8 7 6 5 4 3 2 1

BRIEF CONTENTS

CONTENTS

LAB 1
DESIGNING THE HARDWARE AND SOFTWARE INFRASTRUCTURE

THIS LAB CONTAINS THE FOLLOWING EXERCISES AND ACTIVITIES:

Exercise 1.1   Using Windows System Monitor to Assess Current Disk Throughput

Exercise 1.2   Forecasting Future Disk Storage Requirements

Exercise 1.3   Gathering Information about Database Servers

Exercise 1.4   Using System Monitor to Assess Memory Requirements

Exercise 1.1	Using Windows System Monitor to Assess Current Disk Throughput
Scenario	As the lead database administrator for your company, you understand how important it is to keep SQL Server up and running at top speed. You want to make sure all the subsystems on the server are working in harmony and none are being overloaded. The best way to accomplish that goal is to view the data in Windows System Monitor on a regular basis.
Duration	This task should take approximately 15 minutes.
Setup	For this task, you need access to a machine configured with a default instance SQL Server.
Caveat	You must have administrative privileges on Windows Server 2003.

Procedure	In this task, you will work with the graph and report views in Windows System Monitor.
Equipment Used	For this task, you need access to a machine on which Windows Server 2003 is installed.
Objective	To work with Windows System Monitor.
Criteria for Completion	This task is complete when you have familiarized yourself with Windows System Monitor.

■ PART A: Using Windows System Monitor to Assess Current Disk Throughput

1. Click **Start**, select **Run**, and then type **perfmon** in the text box.

2. System Monitor (Figure 1-1) opens. By default, it displays a line graph of Pages/sec, Avg. Disk Queue Length, and % Processor Time.

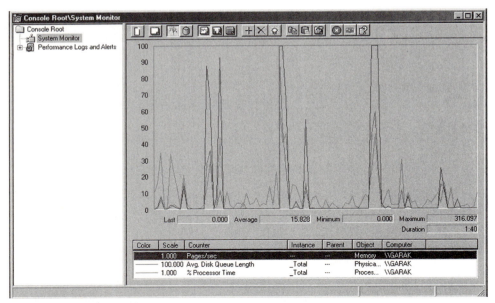

Figure 1-1
System Monitor

3. To assess the current disk throughput, select relevant counters and log the result. In this exercise, you'll remove the Pages/sec and % Processor Time counters. Highlight each counter, and press the **Delete** key on your keyboard.

4. Right click **Avg. Disk Queue Length**, and select **Add Counters** from the pop-up context menu. The Add Counters dialog box opens.

5. In the Performance object drop-down box, select the value **PhysicalDisk**, and then highlight **% Disk Read Time**.

6. While holding down the **Ctrl** key, select **% Disk Write Time** as shown in Figure 1-2.

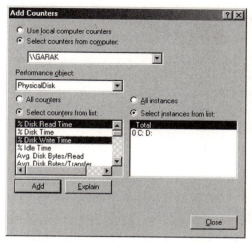

Figure 1-2
Add Counters Dialog Box

7. Click **Add**. Click **Close**.

8. Note that there are three counters showing in System Monitor (Figure 1-3). Perform some simple tasks, such as opening or closing programs to generate disk activity, and watch how the counters change. Don't be alarmed or surprised if one or more of the counters reaches 100% for a short time.

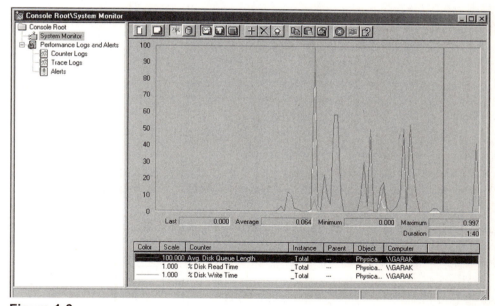

Figure 1-3
System Monitor Showing Disk Counters and Activity

9. Although you can sit there and look at the table for hours to detect trends and periods of peak usage, it's not very practical. In order to be able to make decisions regarding disk usage, you should collect log data over time. To do so, expand the **Performance Logs and Alerts** node in the left window pane.

10. Right click **Counter Logs**, and choose **New Log Settings** from the pop-up menu.

11. Name the new log settings **CurrentDiskThroughputExample**. Click **OK**.

12. Click the **Add Counters** button to open the Add Counters dialog box. Select **PhysicalDisk** from the Performance object drop-down box. While holding down the **Ctrl** key, select **% Disk Read Time, % Disk Write Time**, and **Avg. Disk Queue Length**.

13. Click **Add**. Click **Close**. Note that you can set the interval sampling time in the Sample data every section (see Figure 1-4). The sample period will depend on the item you're measuring and how large a log file you wish to have. One key consideration is that the monitoring consumes resources and may as a result produce skewed readings, especially when monitoring the local computer. Click the **Configure** button on the Log Files tab to open a separate dialog box where you can specify the log file name, folder, and size. Click **Cancel** to close the Configure Log Files dialog box.

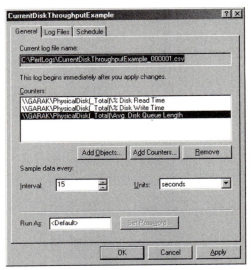

Figure 1-4
The General Tab of the Counter Dialog Box

14. Click the **Log Files** tab. In this window, you can set the log-file type and make other configuration changes. The default log-file type is Binary. For this exercise, change the type to **Text File (Comma Delimited)**.

15. Click the **Schedule** tab. By default, the log file starts as soon as you click Apply or OK and runs until you stop it. Using this dialog box, you can set logging to start at a particular time and date and stop after a specified interval or at a time or date.

16. Click **OK**. If the specified folder doesn't exist, you receive a warning and are given the opportunity to let the program create the folder (Figure 1-5). Click **Yes.**

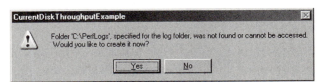

Figure 1-5
Warning Message with Create Option

17. Let the program run for a few minutes. You can force disk activity by opening and closing programs, creating and deleting files, and performing other basic disk subsystem tasks.

18. After no less than three minutes, click the **Counter Logs** node in the left pane of System Monitor. Highlight **CurrentDiskThroughputExample**. Right click, and select **Stop** from the context menu to end logging (Figure 1-6). Note that the icon turns red to indicate "stopped."

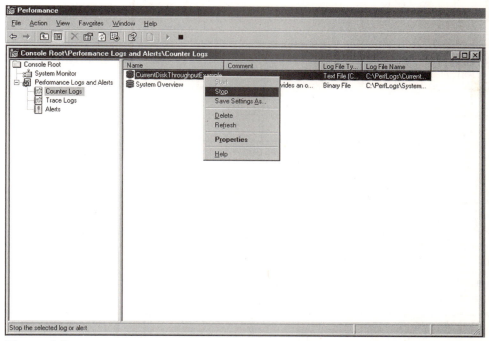

Figure 1-6
Counter Log with Context Menu and Stop Highlighted

19. Navigate to the folder where the log file is located. You can open it with Notepad, but you'll find that CSV files work best with Excel. If you chose the SQL Database log-file type, you can open the database with SQL Server.

Question 1	*Explain the meaning of each counter and how the counters relate to describing the system's current needs. Hint: Did you notice the Explain button on the Add Counters dialog box? Is there a difference between instances? Another hint: Instance in this context means a counter subset not a SQL Server additional installation.*

Exercise 1.2	Forecasting Future Disk Storage Requirements
Scenario	You've been employed by the Yanni HealthCare Services Network to help modify the existing database server infrastructure. The company currently uses 600 GB of disk storage. A review of company plans and relevant regulatory requirements related to HIPAA leads you to conclude that the company will experience a 2% increase per month through the four-year life of the estimation period.
Duration	This task should take approximately 15 minutes.
Setup	There are no configuration requirements.
Caveat	This task doesn't have any caveats.
Procedure	Calculate the expected disk space requirement at the midpoint and end of the estimation period. How much extra disk space will be required beyond the current levels?
Equipment Used	There are no equipment requirements.
Objective	To understand capacity planning methods.
Criteria for Completion	This task is complete when you have calculated the anticipated capacity requirements.

■ PART A: Forecasting Future Disk Storage Requirements

1. This is an example of compound growth, so apply the formula $F = C \times (1 + R)^{\wedge}T$, where the following is true:

    F = Future disk space

    C = Current disk space

    T = Growth rate time unit

    R = Rate of growth

2. To assess the need at the midpoint, set $C = 600$, $T = 24$, and $R = .02$.

3. $F = 600 \times (1 + .02)^{\wedge}24$. So F is 965 GB. This is an extra disk-space requirement of 365 GB at the midpoint (two-year point).

4. To assess the need at the end of the period, set the formula values to $F = 600 \times (1.02)^{\wedge}48$, which is 1552 GB or 952 GB extra disk space needed by the end of four years. As you can see, because of the compounding effect, almost twice as much disk space will be required in the second half of the period than at the beginning.

Exercise 1.3	Gathering Information about Database Servers
Scenario	As the lead database administrator for your company, you understand how important it is to keep SQL Server up and running at top speed. You want to make sure all the subsystems on the server are working in harmony and none are being overloaded. The best way to accomplish that goal is to view the data in Windows System Monitor on a regular basis.
Duration	This task should take approximately 15 minutes.
Setup	For this task, you need access to a machine configured with SQL Server developer or enterprise editions.
Caveat	This task doesn't have any caveats.
Procedure	In this task you examine Configuration Manager and check Books Online for the consequences of system settings.
Equipment Used	For this task, you need access to a machine on which SQL Server is installed.
Objective	To work with SQL Server Configuration Manager.
Criteria for Completion	This task is complete when you have familiarized yourself with SQL Server Configuration Manager.

■ PART A: Gathering Information about Database Servers

1. Select **Start** then **Programs** then **Microsoft SQL Server** then **Configuration Tools** then **SQL Server Configuration Manager**.

2. In the leftmost pane of the SQL Server Configuration Manager dialog box, select **SQL Server Services** to display the list of installed services on each instance and their current state.

3. Select **SQL Server Network Configuration**, and select any instance (Figure 1-7). The rightmost pane shows a list of installed network protocols and their status.

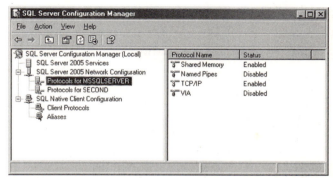

Figure 1-7
SQL Server Configuration Manager

Exercise 1.4	Using System Monitor to Assess Memory Requirements
Scenario	Your SQL server is running slowly. You suspect that the server is running low on RAM memory. You need to get a better understanding of what is occurring with regard to memory.
Duration	This task should take approximately 15 minutes.
Setup	For this task, you need access to a machine configured with a default instance of SQL Server.
Caveat	You must have administrative privileges on Windows Server 2003.
Procedure	In this task you will work with graph and report views in Windows System Monitor.
Equipment Used	For this task, you need access to a machine on which Windows Server 2003 is installed.
Objective	To work with Windows System Monitor.
Criteria for Completion	This task is complete when you have familiarized yourself with Windows System Monitor.

■ PART A: Using System Monitor to Assess Memory Requirements

1. Click **Start**, select **Run**, and type **perfmon.msc** in the text box.

2. System Monitor opens. By default, it displays a line graph of Pages/sec, Avg. Disk Queue Length, and % Processor Time.

3. To assess the current memory throughput, you should select relevant counters and log the result. In this exercise, using the procedures you learned in Exercise 1.1, use System Monitor to log the following counters for the default instance of SQL Server in a file named **CurrentMemoryUsage**:

    - Memory:Available Bytes
    - Memory:Pages/sec
    - SQLServer:Memory Manager:Total Server Memory
    - Process:Working Set
    - SQLServer:Buffer Manager:Buffer Cache Hit Ratio
    - SQLServer:Buffer Manager:Page Life Expectancy

4. Allow logging to run for five minutes.

5. After no less than five minutes, click the **Counter Logs** node in the left pane of System Monitor. Highlight **CurrentMemoryUsage**. Right click, and select **Stop** from the context menu to end logging. Note that the icon turns red to indicate "stopped." Review the contents of the log file as you did earlier.

LAB 2
DESIGNING PHYSICAL STORAGE

THIS LAB CONTAINS THE FOLLOWING EXERCISES AND ACTIVITIES:

Exercise 2.1	Estimating Table Size
Exercise 2.2	Shrinking a Transaction Log File
Exercise 2.3	Examining the Location of System Database Files
Exercise 2.4	Modifying tempdb Size and Growth Parameters
Exercise 2.5	Using Configuration Manager

Exercise 2.1	Estimating Table Size
Scenario	Assume you've completed planning and decided to create a sales database that will contain three tables: one for customer information, one for product information, and one for order detail information. You decide to calculate how large the new database will be when filled with data, which you estimate will be 10,000 records.
Duration	This task should take approximately 15 minutes.
Setup	There are no configuration requirements.
Caveat	This task doesn't have any caveats.
Procedure	This is a paper and pencil—and, perhaps, calculator—effort.
Equipment Used	There are no equipment requirements.
Objective	To understand capacity planning methods.

Criteria for Completion	This task is complete when you have calculated the anticipated capacity requirements.

■ PART A: Estimating Table Size

1. To determine how large the customer table is, add all the field sizes in the table. Here is the table layout (you should get 125 bytes):

custid	int
fname	varchar(20)
lname	varchar(20)
address	varchar(50)
city	varchar(20)
state	char(2)
zip	char(9)

NOTE	*Datatype int uses 4 bytes of storage. Each row also has some overhead which is ignored for this approximation.*

2. Divide 8,096 (the amount of data a single page can hold) by 125, and round down to the nearest number to find out how many of these rows can fit on a single data page. You must round down in every case because a row can't span a page. The answer is 64.

3. Divide 10,000 (the estimated number of rows in the table) by the number of rows on a page (64), and round up to the nearest number. You round up here because a partial row will be moved to a whole new page—there is no such thing as a partial page of storage. The answer is 157.

4. Multiply 157 (the number of pages required to hold 10,000 records) by 8,192 (the size of a page on disk). This is 1,286,144 bytes.

5. With 10,000 records, the customer table in your sales database will require approximately 1.3 MB of hard disk space. By repeating these steps for each table in the database, you can figure out approximately how much space to allocate to the database when you first create it.

Exercise 2.2	Shrinking a Transaction Log File
Scenario	You read that SQL Server will shut down if it runs out of log storage space on disk. You become concerned because there is no evidence your predecessor ever managed file consumption. You run DBCC SQLPERF(LogSpace) and discover your system is using 97% of the log space allocated. You decide to shrink the log file.
Duration	This task should take approximately 15 minutes.
Setup	For this task, you need access to a machine on which SQL Server is installed.

Caveat	You must be a member of the SQL Server sysadmin role to manipulate files.
Procedure	You'll shrink the AdventureWorks database transaction log file by using Management Studio. Check Books Online for other methods.
Equipment Used	For this task, you need access to a machine on which SQL Server is installed.
Objective	To understand the importance of log file maintenance.
Criteria for Completion	This task is complete when you have successfully reduced the log file size.

■ **PART A: Shrinking a Transaction Log File**

1. From the Start menu, select **All Programs** then **Microsoft SQL Server** then **SQL Server Management Studio**.

2. In Object Explorer, connect to a SQL Server Database Engine instance, and then expand that instance.

3. Expand **Databases**, and then right click the **AdventureWorks** database.

4. Point to **Tasks**, point to **Shrink**, and then click **Files**.

5. Set **File Type** to **Log**, using the drop-down box (see Figure 2-1).

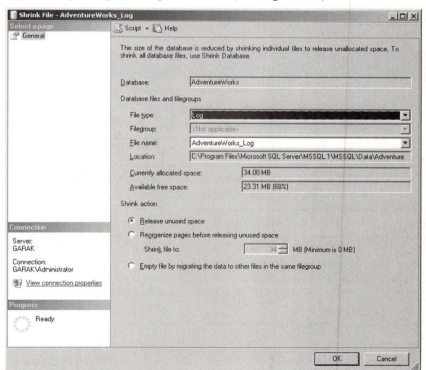

Figure 2-1
Shrink File

6. Choose from the following Shrink action options:

   a. Selecting the **Release unused space** check box causes any unused space in the file to be released to the operating system and shrinks the file to the last allocated extent. This reduces the file size without moving any data.

   b. Selecting the **Reorganize pages before releasing unused space** check box requires you to specify the Shrink file to value. By default, the option is cleared. This option causes any unused space in the file to be released to the operating system and tries to relocate rows to unallocated pages. If you select **Reorganize pages before releasing unused space**, you can enter the maximum percentage of free space to be left in the database file after the database has been shrunk. Permissible values are between 0 and 99.

   c. Selecting the **Empty file by migrating the data to other files in the same filegroup** check box moves all data from the specified file to other files in the filegroup. The empty file can then be deleted.

7. Click **OK**.

NOTE	You can also use the DBCC SHRINKFILE T-SQL command to shrink a file. DBCC SHRINKDATABASE can be used to shrink an entire database.

Question 1	There is also a database option of Auto Shrink. Compare and contrast these three methods. Which would you use when?

Exercise 2.3	Examining the Location of System Database Files
Scenario	You have become concerned that your database is growing fast enough that you will exceed your system disk capacity in a few months. You want to know what will be impacted. Where are the log and data files stored?
Duration	This task should take approximately 15 minutes.
Setup	For this task, you need access to a machine on which a default instance of SQL Server developer or enterprise editions is installed.
Caveat	There are no caveats for this exercise.
Procedure	You'll locate and examine the various system database files using Windows Explorer and Books Online.
Equipment Used	For this task, you need access to a machine on which SQL Server is installed.
Objective	To investigate the file systems used by SQL Server.
Criteria for Completion	This task is complete when you have located the stipulated files.

■ PART A: Examining the Location of System Database Files

1. Open **My Computer** and navigate to Program Files\Microsoft SQL Server\MSSQL.1\MSSQL\Data.

2. Find an example of each of the following objects, and note the storage locations of each with the size, if available:

   Resource database

   Master database

   Model database

   Backups

   Full-text indexes

   Stored procedures

> **NOTE**
>
> *Views, rules default constraint, trigger, check constraint, and stored procedures are all stored in a metadata table.*

3. Close any open instances of SQL Server.
4. Wait a minute, and then restart SQL Server.

> **NOTE**
>
> *This does **not** mean rebooting the operating system.*

5. Return to Program Files\Microsoft SQL Server\MSSQL.1\MSSQL\Data.
6. Select **View** then **Refresh** from the menu bar.
7. Record the sizes of the files in step 2, and compare them with the previous entries. Which, if any, have changed?

Exercise 2.4	Modifying tempdb Size and Growth Parameters
Scenario	Assume you've completed planning and decided to create a sales database that will contain three tables: one for customer information, one for product information, and one for order detail information. You decide to calculate how large the new database will be when filled with data, which you estimate will be 10,000 records. You now turn your attention to the storage needs of tempdb. How large is it now? Should it be allowed to grow without boundaries?
Duration	This task should take approximately 15 minutes.
Setup	For this task, you need access to a machine on which a default instance of SQL Server is installed.

Caveat	You must have administrative privileges on Windows Server.
Procedure	You'll reset the tempdb size and growth parameters. Check "Deciding on the tempdb Database Physical Storage" in your textbook.
Equipment Used	For this task, you need access to a machine on which SQL Server is installed.
Objective	To understand tempdb's space requirements.
Criteria for Completion	This task is complete when you know how much space is used by tempdb.

■ PART A: Modifying tempdb Size and Growth Parameters

1. From the Start menu, select **All Programs** then **Microsoft SQL Server** then **SQL Server Management Studio**.
2. In Object Explorer, connect to a SQL Server Database Engine instance, and then expand that instance.
3. Expand **Databases**, and then open the **System Databases** folder. Select **tempdb**, right click it, and then click **Properties**.
4. In Database Properties, select the **Files** page (Figure 2-2).

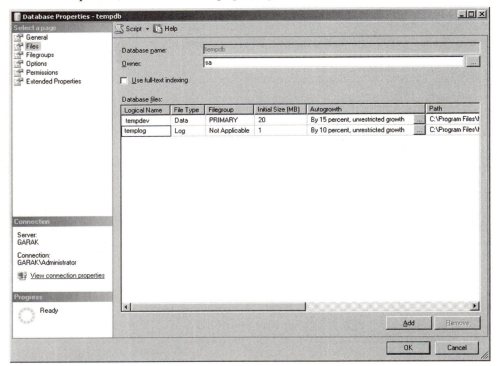

Figure 2-2
Files Page of Database Properties

5. Select the **tempdev** file, and increase the initial size to a value of your choice by modifying the value in the Initial Size (MB) column. You must increase the size of the database by at least 1 MB.

6. Click the **ellipsis button** under the Autogrowth column to open the Change Autogrowth dialog box. Reset file growth to 15 percent. Note that you can use this window to disable autogrowth, set file-growth measures to percentages or MBs. You can also allow unrestricted file growth or restrict it to a certain size. Click **OK**.

7. Verify that your changes have been entered. Click **OK**.

NOTE	*Changes made to the setting for the size and file-growth increment take effect immediately after restarting the instance of SQL Server.*

Exercise 2.5	Using Configuration Manager
Scenario	You're the database manager at your company. A junior administrator, having an inquiring mind, asked you: "What is Configuration Manager. Is that a way to get administrative privileges into the Windows Server operating system?" How do you respond?
Duration	This task should take approximately 15 minutes.
Setup	For this task, you need access to a machine on which a default instance of SQL Server developer or enterprise edition is installed.
Caveat	There are no special considerations for this exercise.
Procedure	You'll use the Configuration Manager to start and stop the default instance of SQL Server. Use Books Online to investigate aspects you don't yet understand.
Equipment Used	For this task, you need access to a machine on which SQL Server is installed.
Objective	To understand the need for and the purposes of a Configuration Manager utility.
Criteria for Completion	This task is complete when you have familiarized yourself with SQL Server Configuration Manager.

■ PART A: Using Configuration Manager

To start the default instance of SQL Server from Configuration Manager, do the following:

1. From the Start menu, select **All Programs** then **Microsoft SQL Server** then **Configuration Tools** then **SQL Server Configuration Manager**.

2. In SQL Server Configuration Manager select **SQL Server Services**.

3. In the details pane, right click **SQL Server (MSSQLServer)**, and then click **Start**. If Start is grayed out because SQL Server (MSSQLServer) is set to run automatically, click **Restart** instead. This will stop and restart the service.

4. A green arrow on the icon next to the server name and on the toolbar indicates that the server started successfully.

5. Click **Close** to terminate SQL Server Configuration Manager.

> **NOTE**
>
> *The SQL Server database engine functions as a service.*

LAB 3
DESIGNING A CONSOLIDATION STRATEGY

THIS LAB CONTAINS THE FOLLOWING EXERCISES AND ACTIVITIES:

Exercise 3.1   Gathering Performance Information over Time

Exercise 3.1	Gathering Performance Information over Time
Scenario	You are the database administrator for a small company with large aspirations. You experience constant growth and you feel you need to keep track of these additional pressures on your SQL Server Instance. You decide to gather performance statistics over a period of months.
Duration	This task should take approximately 15 minutes.
Setup	For this task, you need access to a machine on which a default instance of SQL Server is installed.
Caveat	You need administrative privilege access to the server operating system.
Procedure	You'll gather and review a number of performance-related metrics from one of your SQL Server instances.
Equipment Used	For this task, you need access to a machine on which a default instance of SQL Server is installed.
Objective	To work with Windows System Monitor.
Criteria for Completion	This task is complete when you have familiarized yourself with Performance Monitor and Alerts.

■ PART A: Gathering Performance Information over Time

1. Click **Start** then **Administrative Tools**, and choose the **Performance Monitor** application. The Performance application automatically starts the System Monitor (Figure 3-1).

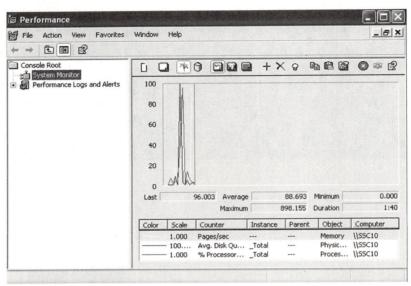

Figure 3-1
System Monitor

2. When Performance Monitor opens, expand the **Performance Logs and Alerts** section, and choose **Counter Logs** (Figure 3-2).

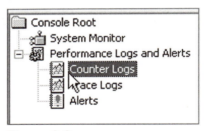

Figure 3-2
Performance Logs and Alerts

3. Right click the **Counter Logs** item, and select **New Log Settings** from the menu that appears. Enter a name for the performance data. Click **OK**. It's recommended that you include the date in your name. The **General** tab of the main dialog appears (Figure 3-3), where you can choose your counters.

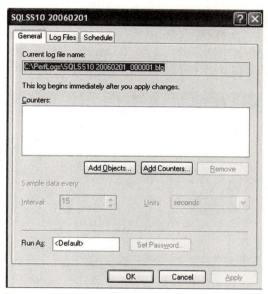

Figure 3-3
The General Tab of the Counter Dialog Box

4. Click the **Add Counters** button to get the list of counters. The Add Counters dialog box (Figure 3-4) appears. The local computer is the default, but you can change it to monitor a remote computer. Select the Performance object, the counter, and instance needed. In this case, choose the **tempdb** instance of the **Data File(s) Size (KB)** counter for the **SQLServer:Databases** object. When you click **Add**, this counter is added to your list, but the dialog box doesn't close. Continue to explore and add counters until you reach of total of ten.

Figure 3-4
The Add Counters Dialog Box

5. Once you've added all your counters to the list, click the **Close** button to return to the main counter dialog box. You can change the sample rate using the Interval spinner. It's recommended you only monitor every 5 to 15 minutes for trending data.

6. Click the **Log Files** tab at the top to see the details of the file storage type (Figure 3-5). Change this to **Text File (Comma delimited)**, which lets you load this data easily into Excel. You can also choose a plain-text file or an SQL database. You can also change the default file location using the Configure button.

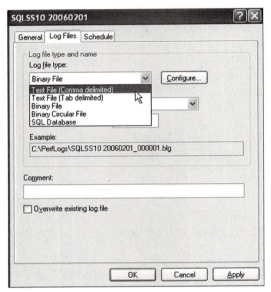

Figure 3-5
The Log Files Tab of the Counter Dialog Box

7. Click the **Schedule** tab (see Figure 3-6), and select a stop time of after one minute. You can also schedule this if Performance Monitor is running on your server.

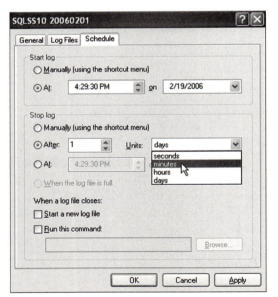

Figure 3-6
The Schedule Tab of the Counter Dialog Box

8. Click the **OK** button, and the trace will begin if set to do so. When a trace is running, it appears with a green icon beside it (Figure 3-7).

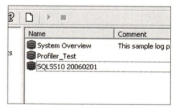

Figure 3-7
A Portion of the System Monitor Window

9. Navigate to the file location where your trace data was stored, and open the .csv file with a text editor. In this case, you can see that five data points were recorded (Figure 3-8) if you left the interval unchanged in step 5.

```
"(PDH-CSV 4.0) (Mountain Standard Time)(420)","\\SSC10\SQLServer:Databases(tempdb)\Data File(s) Size (KB)"
"02/19/2006 16:41:18.937","8192"
"02/19/2006 16:41:33.937","8192"
"02/19/2006 16:41:48.937","8192"
"02/19/2006 16:42:03.937","8192"
"02/19/2006 16:42:18.937","8192"
```

Figure 3-8
Example Trace Log Results

Question 1	SQL Server Profiler also collects performance information over time. Compare and contrast the tools. Which would you use when?

LAB 4
ANALYZING AND DESIGNING SECURITY

THIS LAB CONTAINS THE FOLLOWING EXERCISES AND ACTIVITIES:

Exercise 4.1   Analyzing the Time Cost of Password Resets

Exercise 4.2   Changing Authentication Modes

Exercise 4.1	Analyzing the Time Cost of Password Resets
Scenario	You've decided that your SQL Server 2005 servers will all be installed on Windows 2003 servers and use the integrated password policy available with this operating system. Based on historical information from your help desk, you expect 2.3 password-reset requests per employee per year. The average time to respond to an open request such as this is 30 minutes, and a technician requires about 5 minutes to complete this task, including contacting the individual and documenting the change.
Duration	This task should take approximately 15 minutes.
Setup	No special equipment is required for this task.
Caveat	This task has no caveats.
Procedure	You'll calculate the cost of implementing this request for 10 people if the average salary for your employees is $60,000 per year.
Equipment Used	Paper, pencil and, perhaps, a calculator.
Objective	To understand the financial consequences of business process decisions.
Criteria for Completion	This task is complete when you have familiarized yourself with one policy enforcement consequence.

■ PART A: Analyzing the Time Cost of Password Resets

1. Divide the salary per year by the number of hours worked per year. This is the cost per hour.
2. Divide the cost per hour by 2 to calculate the cost of the 30 minutes it takes to change a password.
3. Multiply this number by the number of resets you expect: 2.3 per person. This is the cost per employee.
4. Multiply this number by the number of employees. This gives us the total cost of the lost work for the company while employees wait on password resets.
5. To determine the cost for the help desk to perform the tasks, divide the cost of an employee per hour (the result from step 1) by the number of password resets that can be performed per hour.
6. Multiply this result by the number of requests from step 3 to get the cost to the help desk for performing the resets.
7. Add the results of step 4 and step 6 to get the total cost to the organization for this security decision.

Here is the formula for this example:

1. Employee cost per hour: $60,000 per year ÷ 2,000 hours of work per year = $30.00 per hour
2. Employee cost per person: $30.00 ÷ 2 (30 minutes) = $15.00
3. Employee cost per year: $15.00 × 2.3 requests = $34.50
4. Total employee cost: $34.50 × 10 employees = $345.00
5. Help desk cost per request: $30.00 ÷ 12 (twelve 5-minute time slices per hour) = $2.50
6. Total help desk cost: $2.50 × 2.3 requests = $5.75
7. Total employee and help desk cost of this change: $345.00 + $5.75 = $350.75.

Exercise 4.2	Changing Authentication Modes
Scenario	You're the database administrator. You support both a sales team that favors Excel and other Microsoft tools and a marketing team that favors Apple graphics-based tools. Both groups need access to your database: the first to manage the sales strategy from moment-to-moment and the second to prepare dynamic online catalogs.
Duration	This task should take approximately 10 minutes.
Setup	For this task, you need access to a machine on which a default instance of SQL Server is installed.
Caveat	There are no special warnings or conditions for this exercise.
Procedure	Use Management Studio to set the authentication mode.
Equipment Used	For this task, you need access to a machine on which a default instance of SQL Server is installed.
Objective	To configure authentication to support both Windows and non-Windows clients.

Criteria for Completion	This task is complete when you have familiarized yourself with the process to change authentication modes.

■ PART A: Changing Authentication Modes

You choose the authentication mode when SQL Server is installed, but you can also change it later.

1. Select a server in SQL Server Management Studio's Object Explorer, and right click it.
2. Choose **Properties** (Figure 4-1).

Figure 4-1
Object Explorer with Properties of the Instance Selected

3. When the Server Properties dialog box appears, select the **Security** page from the left pane (Figure 4-2).

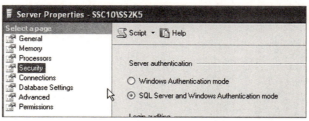

Figure 4-2
A Portion of the Instance Properties Window

4. The top section contains two radio buttons that show your options for authentication. Choose **mixed (SQL Server and Windows Authentication)** mode.
5. Restart the SQL Server service.
6. Close the properties page.

Question 1	*Why did you have stop and restart SQL Server service?*

LAB 5
DESIGNING WINDOWS SERVER-LEVEL SECURITY PROCESSES

THIS LAB CONTAINS THE FOLLOWING EXERCISES AND ACTIVITIES:

Exercise 5.1 Adding a Login to SQL Server

Exercise 5.2 Setting Up a Master Database Encryption Key

Exercise 5.3 Calculating Encrypted Data Size

Exercise 5.4 Exploring Service Account Groups and Changing Ownership

Exercise 5.5 Disabling Integration Services

Exercise 5.1	Adding a Login to SQL Server
Scenario	You've just installed a new SQL Server instance on your development machine to begin testing a customer relationship management (CRM) application. This application uses a single logon for all users, and you decide to add the login CRM_Application_User to your server. You also need to allow the graphic illustrators in the Marketing Department using Apple computers to access the database.
Duration	This task should take approximately 15 minutes.
Setup	For this task, you need access to a machine on which SQL Server is installed.
Caveat	You must have administrative privileges on Windows Server.
Procedure	In this task, you will use Management Studio to create a login.

Equipment Used	For this task, you need access to a machine on which SQL Server is installed.
Objective	To work with Management Studio and logins.
Criteria for Completion	This task is complete when you have familiarized yourself with the login creation process.

■ PART A: Adding a SQL Server Login

1. Right click the **Logins** item under the **Security** folder in Management Studio, and select **New Login** (Figure 5-1).

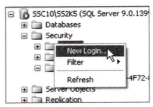

Figure 5-1
A Portion of Management Studio Showing the New Login Selection

2. In the Login Name dialog box that appears (Figure 5-2), enter the user name, select **SQL Server authentication**, enter a password, and confirm that password.

Figure 5-2
New Login Dialog Box

3. Because this login is used by the application and not a physical user, you decide that the password expiration and the requirement to change the password at the next login don't apply, so you deselect them.

4. Click **OK**, and your new login is ready for permissions to be assigned in the appropriate database.

■ PART B: Testing the New User Connection

1. Log in as your new user by clicking **Connect** in Object Explorer and choose **Database Engine**.
2. In the Authentication text box in the Connect to Server dialog box, be sure to choose **SQL Server Authentication** from the drop-down list.
3. Enter the user name and password for the employee you just authorized earlier and click **Connect**.

■ PART C: Controlling Database Access

1. Examine the database to which this user connects. If it's Master you might want to change access to a more appropriate database—for the classroom, consider AdventureWorks.

■ PART D: Reverting to Administrative Privileges

1. Log off as user. Log back on as a user with administrative control.

Exercise 5.2	Setting Up a Master Database Encryption Key
Scenario	You decide you need to guard data even from those who have proper access to your database. The first step is to create a master database encryption key.
Duration	This task should take approximately 15 minutes.
Setup	For this task, you need access to a machine on which a default instance of SQL Server is installed.
Caveat	No special warnings or conditions for this exercise.
Procedure	To encrypt data in a database, you must first create a database master key. You'll create one in the AdventureWorks sample database that comes with SQL Server.
Equipment Used	For this task, you need access to a machine on which SQL Server is installed.
Objective	To understand the procedure to encrypt database information.
Criteria for Completion	This task is complete when you have familiarized yourself with the encryption process.

■ PART A: Setting Up a Master Database Encryption Key

1. Open a new query session in SQL Server Management Studio, and type the following (substituting your own password for the value of "MyP@ssword"):

```
USE AdventureWorks;
GO
CREATE MASTER KEY ENCRYPTION BY PASSWORD = 'MyP@ssword';
GO
```

2. It's also recommended that you encrypt a copy of this key using the service master key. Doing so enables SQL Server to automatically open this key and use it for further encryption operations. Use the following:

```
ALTER MASTER KEY ADD ENCRYPTION BY SERVICE MASTER KEY;
```

Exercise 5.3	Calculating Encrypted Data Size
Scenario	You're working for MySecretShop, an online retailer that specializes in spy equipment for industrial protection. Your boss is concerned that your data could be stolen and wants it encrypted. You agree that credit card data should be encrypted, but you think client names and other information shouldn't be because of the data size.
Duration	This task should take approximately 15 minutes.
Setup	There are no special requirements.
Caveat	There are no warnings or previous requirements.
Procedure	This is a paper, pencil, and perhaps calculator exercise.
Equipment Used	None.
Objective	To understand the increase in storage requirements when encryption is needed.
Criteria for Completion	This task is complete when you have familiarized yourself with the consequences of encrypting domain data.

■ PART A: Calculating Encrypted Data Size

1. To show the impact, you analyze your existing data and determine the storage space is 20 characters for names.

2. With a Triple DES algorithm and an authenticator, you determine the new data size would be as follows:

```
SIZE = (FLOOR ((8 + DATA + (AUTHENTICATOR * 20))/BLOCK) + 1) *
BLOCK + 16 + BLOCK + 4;
```

```
SIZE = (FLOOR ((8 + 20 + (1 * 20))/8) + 1) * 8 + 16 + 8 + 4;
SIZE = (FLOOR ((28 + 20)/8) + 1) * 8 + 28;
SIZE = (FLOOR (6) + 1) * 8 + 28;
SIZE = 7 * 8 + 28;
SIZE = 84;
```

Exercise 5.4	Exploring Service Account Groups and Changing Ownership
Scenario	You're preparing to upgrade a SQL Server 2000 server to SQL Server 2005. On your test server, named <YourServerName>, you've installed SQL Server 2000 along with a named instance of SQL Server 2005, <YourInstanceName>. After adding the SQL Server 2005 instance to SQL Server 2000, you want to check which service accounts have changed. You've installed only SQL Server and SQL Agent services for each instance.
Duration	This task should take approximately 10 minutes.
Setup	For this task, you need access to a machine on which multiple instances of SQL Server 2005 are installed.
Caveat	If you haven't already done so, add a named instance of SQL Server 2005. Use an intuitively obvious name like Instance1. Load FullText service on Instance1. Create a Windows Server user account that you can remember.
Procedure	Use Configuration Manager to investigate which services are loaded and which are running.
Equipment Used	For this task, you need access to a machine on which SQL Server 2005 is installed.
Objective	To work with Configuration Manager and services.
Criteria for Completion	This task is complete when you understand service ownership.

■ PART A: Exploring Service Account Groups

1. Right click **My Computer** on the desktop, and select **Manage**.
2. When the MMC dialog box opens, select the **Local Users and Groups** item and then the **Groups** folder. In this folder, you'll see groups with names similar to the following:
   - **MSSQLServer.** The service account for the SQL Server relational engine of the default instance
   - **SQLServer2005MSSQLUser$SQLTestDEN01$SS2K5.** The service account for the SQL Server relational engine of the named instance
   - **SQLServerAgent.** The SQL Server Agent service account for the default instance
   - **SQLServer2005SQLAgentUser$SQLTestDEN01$SS2K5.** The service account for the named instance's SQL Server Agent

■ PART B: Changing the Service Account

1. Open **SQL Server Services** in **Configuration Manager**. Your screen should look something like Figure 5-3.

Name	State	Start Mode	Log On As		Process ID	Service Type
SQL Server Integration Services	Running	Automatic	NT AUTHORITY\NetworkService		1972	SSIS Server
SQL Server FullText Search (SS2K5)	Running	Automatic	.\S2K5		856	Full Text
SQL Server (SS2K5)	Running	Automatic	.\S2K5		484	SQL Server
SQL Server Agent (SS2K5)	Running	Automatic	.\SS2K5Agent		1824	SQL Agent
SQL Server Browser	Running	Automatic	.\S2K5		672	SQL Browser

Figure 5-3
Viewing SQL Server Services in Configuration Manager

2. Right click the **SQL Server FullText Search** service account and select **Properties**, or double click the **SQL Server FullText Search** service, and you'll see the Properties dialog box (Figure 5-4).

Figure 5-4
SQL Server Full-Text Search Properties

3. This dialog box shows you the current service account and other information. You can select the type of account from the drop-down box. You'll see the built-in accounts available (Figure 5-5).

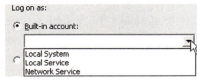

Figure 5-5
Built-In Account Drop-Down Box

4. However, choose another account previously created on your local machine. Type this into the **Account Name** text box and the **Password** for this account into the Password and Confirm Password text boxes. Click **OK**, and you'll see the Confirm Account Change dialog box (Figure 5-6).

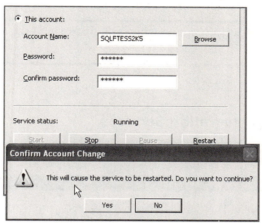

Figure 5-6
Confirm Account Change Dialog Box

The Configuration Manager checks the account name and password and then restarts the service. This logs off the current account running the service and the logs in the new account, which then restarts the service. As you can see in Figure 5-7, the new service account is now running the FullText Search service.

Name	State	Start Mode	Log On As
SQL Server Integration Services	Running	Automatic	NT AUTHORITY\NetworkService
SQL Server FullText Search (SS2K5)	Running	Automatic	.\SQLFTESS2K5
SQL Server (SS2K5)	Running	Automatic	.\S2K5
SQL Server Agent (SS2K5)	Running	Automatic	.\SS2K5Agent
SQL Server Browser	Running	Automatic	.\S2K5

Figure 5-7
Viewing SQL Server Services in Configuration Manager after Change

Exercise 5.5	Disabling Integration Services
Scenario	The data extraction, transformation, and load (ETL) requirements of your company have grown dramatically, and your primary data warehousing server can no longer support the OLTP Server that is running on it in addition to the Integration Services load. You purchase a new server and install OLAP and Integration Services on that server, migrating all your packages to it. You now need to disable the Integration Services service because it's no longer being used on the OLTP server.
Duration	This task should take approximately 10 minutes.
Setup	Assume, as shown in Figure 5-4 in your textbook, that three services are sharing the same user account.
Caveat	No special considerations.

Procedure	You'll use Configuration Manager to disable a service.
Equipment Used	For this task, you need access to a machine on which SQL Server is installed.
Objective	To work with Configuration Manager.
Criteria for Completion	This task is complete when you understand the services.

■ PART A: Disabling Integration Services

1. Start the SQL Server Configuration Manager (Figure 5-8).

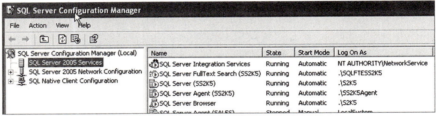

Figure 5-8
SQL Server Configuration Manager

2. Double click the **Integration Services** entry to open the Properties dialog box (Figure 5-9).

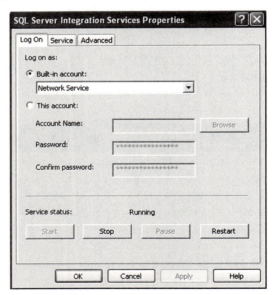

Figure 5-9
SQL Server Integration Services Properties

3.   Select the **Service** tab (Figure 5-10) so you can change the mode for this service.

Figure 5-10
Service Tab of SQL Server Integration Services Properties

4.   On the Service tab, select **Disabled** for the **"Start Mode"** for this service, and click **OK**. This service will no longer start when the server boots.

5.   You need to stop this service, because it will continue to run until the Windows server is restarted. Figure 5-11 illustrates how to do it. Right click the service in the Configuration Manager, and select **Stop**.

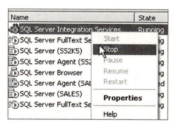

Figure 5-11
A Portion of Configuration Manager Showing Stop Highlighted

LAB 6
DESIGNING SQL SERVER SERVICE-LEVEL AND DATABASE-LEVEL SECURITY

THIS LAB CONTAINS THE FOLLOWING EXERCISES AND ACTIVITIES:

Exercise 6.1   Creating a Login to SQL Server

Exercise 6.2   Adding a User Mapping

Exercise 6.3   Creating a Schema Owned by a User

Exercise 6.4   Adding a User to a Fixed-Database Role

Exercise 6.5   Creating a User-Defined Role

Exercise 6.1	Creating a Login to SQL Server
Scenario	You're the database administrator. You're training a new technician whose first job will be managing user accounts. She must support both Windows and Linux users and manage the permissions through the use of server roles.
Duration	This task should take approximately 15 minutes.
Setup	For this task, you need access to a machine on which a default instance of SQL Server is installed.

Caveat	You need a Windows user account named DelaneyUser. Adding Windows users to the operating system requires administrative privileges. Adding users to SQL Server requires membership in an appropriate server role, such as sysadmin or securityadmin.
Procedure	Use Management Studio to configure user access.
Equipment Used	For this task, you need access to a machine on which SQL Server is installed.
Objective	To work with Management Studio and user accounts.
Criteria for Completion	This task is complete when you have familiarized yourself with server properties of SQL Server.

■ PART A: Creating a Login to SQL Server

1. To create a login to SQL Server, you must first select the **Security** folder in **Management Studio** and then select the **Logins** folder (Figure 6-1).
2. Right click the **Logins** folder, and select **New Login**.

Figure 6-1
A Portion of Management Studio Showing the New Login Selection

3. This opens the Login—New dialog box as shown in Figure 6-2. In this dialog box, select the type of login you want to create: Windows authentication or SQL Server authentication. This example shows a SQL Server login being created, which means you must enter a password and then choose to enforce the password options below that.

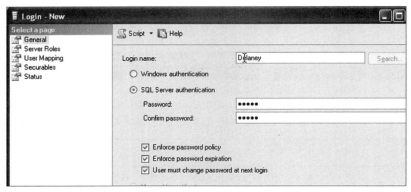

Figure 6-2
New Login Dialog Box—SQL Server Authentication

4. Alternatively, if you change to a Windows-authenticated login, you can enter the domain and user as *domain\user* or click **Search**. When a Windows login is selected, the password as well as policy options are disabled, as shown in Figure 6-3.

Figure 6-3
New Login Dialog Box—Windows Authentication

5. Clicking the Search button opens the standard Windows user/group search dialog box (Figure 6-4) in which you can enter a domain and/or username and verify its existence or select from matching items in Active Directory.

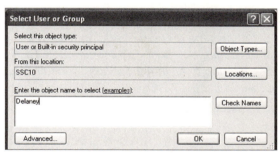

Figure 6-4
Select User or Group Search Dialog Box

6. In this case, return to the SQL Server-authenticated login and add the user **DelaneyUser** with a password of your choosing. You should select the password options because they provide additional levels of security. Note that this login will be used in other exercises in this Lesson.

7. Below these options are two more you can change (as shown in Figure 6-5): the default database and the default language. Selecting the database drop down gives you a list of databases on your server from which you can choose. The default is master; change this to **AdventureWorks** for this example or to any other user database you use for testing.

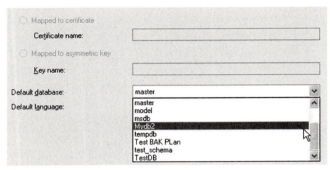

Figure 6-5
Default Database Drop-Down Box

8. The language is set to the server default; however, go ahead and set this to a particular language for any login. If the server default changes later, it won't affect this login. There are also mappings to certificates or asymmetric keys if these already exist in the master database.

> *Exercise 6.1 shows the method of adding a login using SQL Server Management Studio, but the T-SQL command CREATE LOGIN includes commands that map to all these options. Consult SQL Server Books Online for the syntax for T-SQL.*

■ PART B: Adding a Login to a Server Role

1. In Management Studio, connect to your server as a securityadmin or sysadmin login. In a new query editor pane, enter the following:

```
EXEC sp_addsrvrolemember 'DelaneyUser', 'processadmin';
GO
EXEC sp_addsrvrolemember 'DelaneyUser', 'dbcreator';
GO
```

2. Click the **Execute** button to execute this code and add Delaney to these roles.

3. You can check that this process executed correctly with the following:

```
EXEC sp_helpsrvrolemember 'dbcreator';
EXEC sp_helpsrvrolemember 'processadmin';
```

This will return something like the following:

```
ServerRole      MemberName   MemberSID
------------    -----------  --------------------------
Dbcreator       DelaneyUser  0xE896B0CA4536F744BD5C839B
(1 row(s) affected)
```

```
ServerRole      MemberName  MemberSID
----------      ----------- ------------------------
Processadmin    DelaneyUser 0xE896B0CA4536F744BD5C83
(1 row(s) affected)
```

> **NOTE** *The MemberSID column will be different on your sever.*

Exercise 6.2	Adding a User Mapping
Scenario	You're the database administrator. Nancy's Windows login is NESmith, but in her database she prefers to connect as Nancy. Although it's considered a standard practice to have users with the same name as their mapped logins, it isn't necessary.
Duration	This task should take approximately 15 minutes.
Setup	For this task, you need access to a machine on which a default instance of SQL Server is installed.
Caveat	You must have sysadmin privileges on Windows Server.
Procedure	You'll use the DelaneyUser from Exercise 6.1 in this exercise, adding this user to the AdventureWorks database. To do this, you'll use T-SQL again. If you haven't installed the AdventureWorks database, you can use any database on your server, either a system database or one you've created.
Equipment Used	For this task, you need access to a machine on which SQL Server is installed.
Objective	To work with Management Studio and user accounts.
Criteria for Completion	This task is complete when you have familiarized yourself with user aliases (mappings).

■ PART A: Adding a User Mapping

1. In Management Studio, connect to your server as a securityadmin or sysadmin login. In a new query window, enter the following:

```
USE AdventureWorks;
GO
CREATE USER DelaneyUser FOR LOGIN DelaneyUser;
GO
SELECT * FROM sys.database_principals;
GO
```

2. You'll see results similar to those shown in Figure 6-6. Note that the SID for DelaneyUser matches the SID from the server roles in Exercise 6.1B.

	name	principal_id	type	type_desc	defau...	c	o...	sid
1	public	0	R	DATABASE_ROLE	NULL	2	1	0x010500000000000904000000731D6F70B3BF1142820A040...
2	dbo	1	U	WINDOWS_USER	dbo	2	N..	0x0105000000000005150000000D7A5A33FE26C648828BA6...
3	guest	2	S	SQL_USER	guest	2	N..	0x00
4	INFORMATION_SCHEMA	3	S	SQL_USER	NULL	2	N..	NULL
5	sys	4	S	SQL_USER	NULL	2	N..	NULL
6	DelaneyUser	5	S	SQL_USER	dbo	2	N..	0xE896B0CA4536F744BD5C839B537E79C9
7	db_owner	16384	R	DATABASE_ROLE	NULL	2	1	0x01050000000000090400000000000000000000000000000000...

Figure 6-6
Select Results

Exercise 6.3	Creating a Schema Owned by a User
Scenario	You've just installed a new SQL Server instance on your development machine. The programmers wish to start using schema namespace to help with porting old code from multiple previous applications that used the same object names in each. You need to create the schemas so that they can start moving the old code and begin testing.
Duration	This task should take approximately 15 minutes.
Setup	For this task, you need access to a machine on which a default instance of SQL Server is installed.
Caveat	You must be a member of the sysadmin role.
Procedure	You'll use the DelaneyUser user created in Exercise 6.2 in this exercise. Because this will be the user for the primary application, you want to create a schema that will hold the objects for this application.
Equipment Used	For this task, you need access to a machine on which SQL Server is installed.
Objective	To work with Management Studio and understand schema concepts.
Criteria for Completion	This task is complete when you have familiarized yourself with schema namespace purposes.

■ PART A: Creating a Schema Owned by a User

1. Using Management Studio, select a database in the Databases folder, and then expand the database folder and choose **Security**.

2. Right click **Schemas**, and select **New Schema** as shown in Figure 6-7.

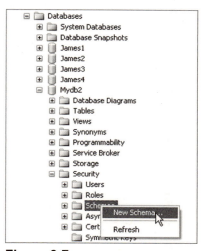

Figure 6-7
A Portion of Management Studio Showing the New Schema Selection

3. In the New Schema dialog box (Figure 6-8), enter **PrimaryApp** for the Schema name in this database.

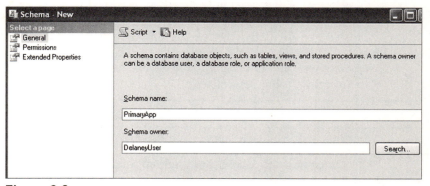

Figure 6-8
New Schema Dialog Box

4. You can either directly enter the username or search for it by clicking the Search button. In this case, enter **DelaneyUser**, and click **OK**. Checking the list of schemas for the database, you'll now see the new schema listed (Figure 6-9).

Figure 6-9
A Portion of Management Studio Showing the PrimaryApp
Schema

Question 1	OK. You created a schema owned by DelaneyUser. Paul gets fired. You want to drop him as a user. You can't. He owns an object. What must you do?

Exercise 6.4	Adding a User to a Fixed-Database Role
Scenario	Nancy needs some analysts using her database to stop updating information. Politely asking them to stop hasn't helped. She would like Amy and Peter added to the db_denydatawriter role. You check with their supervisor who agrees that they require only read access and volunteers to let them know she has approved your actions.
Duration	This task should take approximately 15 minutes.
Setup	For this task, you need access to a machine on which SQL Server is installed.
Caveat	You must have db_owner or sysadmin role membership to make this change.
Procedure	You'll take DelaneyUser from Exercise 6.2 and assign this user to the db_datareader role.
Equipment Used	For this task, you need access to a machine on which SQL Server is installed.
Objective	To work with SQL Server Management Studio and fixed database roles.
Criteria for Completion	This task is complete when you have familiarized yourself with database roles.

■ PART A: Adding a User to a Fixed-Database Role

1. Using the query editor in Management Studio that is connected to the test database, execute the following to add DelaneyUser to the db_datareader role:

```
EXEC sp_addrolemember 'db_datareader', 'DelaneyUser';
```

After executing this statement, you can check the role membership in two places: in the properties for the db_datareader role, as shown in Figure 6-10, or in the properties for DelaneyUser, which shows a check box for the role in the bottom edit box.

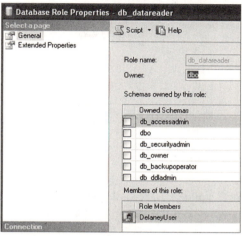

Figure 6-10
Database Role Properties Window

2. To view the properties for the role, expand the **Security** folder under the test database, and choose **Database Roles**. In the right pane, select the role, right click it, and choose **Properties**.

3. To view the properties for the user, expand the **Users** folder under Security, and select the **DelaneyUser** in the right pane. Right click the user, and choose **Properties**.

Exercise 6.5	Creating a User-Defined Role
Scenario	Suppose you have a series of data-entry clerks who use an application to enter new sales invoices and line items. They're allowed to enter new invoices or line items, but they can't delete line items; they can only change them.
Duration	This task should take approximately 15 minutes.
Setup	For this task, you need access to a machine on which SQL Server is installed.
Caveat	You must have appropriate permissions in SQL Server.
Procedure	You'll create a role in this exercise to handle this requirement.
Equipment Used	For this task, you need access to a machine on which SQL Server is installed.
Objective	To work with Management Studio and roles.

Criteria for Completion	This task is complete when you have familiarized yourself with the concept of roles and permission inheritance.

■ PART A: Creating a User-Defined Role

1. Open Management Studio, select your database, select the **Security** folder, and then right click the **Roles** folder and select **New Database Role** (Figure 6-11).

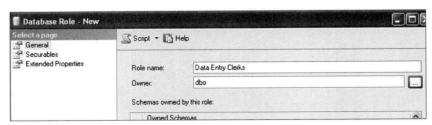

Figure 6-11
New Database Role Dialog Box

2. This opens the Naming the Database Role dialog box (Figure 6-12), where you can enter the name of this role and the owner. Set the name to **"Data Entry Clerks"** and set the owner as **dbo** (or choose another user if your needs require you to do so).

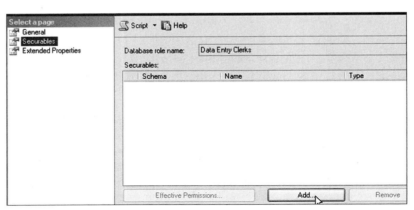

Figure 6-12
Naming the Database Role Dialog Box

3. To add your user to this role, click the **Add** button below the Role Members edit box. This opens the Search dialog box, which allows you to search for a member. In this case, enter the name of the user, **DelaneyUser**.

4. Click **OK**. You're returned to the General screen for the Database Role. As shown in Figure 6-13, the user is now a member of this role.

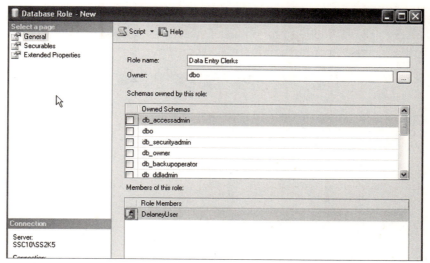

Figure 6-13
New Database Role Dialog Box

5. Once you've done this, you can click the **Securables** folder in the left pane in Figure 6-14. This opens the Securables dialog box. As you can see, there are no permissions assigned in the top edit box by default.

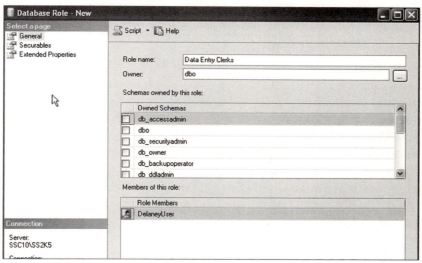

Figure 6-14
New Database Role Dialog Box

6. Click the **Add** button to open the Object Search dialog box (Figure 6-15). You can search for specific objects, specific types, or all objects in a schema. Choose all objects in the dbo schema in this exercise (as shown in Figure 6-16).

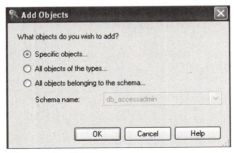

Figure 6-15
Add Objects Window for Specific Objects

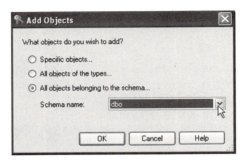

Figure 6-16
Add Objects Belonging to a Particular Schema

7. Choosing the dbo schema loads those tables into the to edit pane of the Database Role Properties dialog box. By clicking a particular object, you can see the permissions for that object. By clicking in the GRANT column, you allow that permission for that object in this role. The WITH GRANT option allows this role's members to grant this permission to others. The DENY column explicitly prevents this role's members from accessing the object. If you removed a checkmark from the GRANT or WITH GRANT column, you would be performing a REVOKE for that permission. For this exercise, grant the INSERT and SELECT permissions, but not the DELETE permission. Also check the UPDATE permission.

8. Click **OK** to set these permissions for this role.

LAB 7
DESIGNING SQL SERVER OBJECT-LEVEL SECURITY

THIS LAB CONTAINS THE FOLLOWING EXERCISES AND ACTIVITIES:

Exercise 7.1   Assiging Permissions to a User Role

Exercise 7.2   Changing Execution Context

Exercise 7.3   Encrypting a Column of Data

Exercise 7.4   Enabling the CLR Environment

Exercise 7.1	Assigning Permissions to a User Role
Scenario	Nancy still has problems with analysts failing to follow her protocols in her database. She has asked you to create a user role for the financial analysts to more carefully control their access.
Duration	This task should take approximately 15 minutes.
Setup	For this task, you need access to a machine on which a default instance of SQL Server is installed.
Caveat	You must be a member of the sysadmin role on SQL Server.
Procedure	In this exercise, you'll create a role in the AdventureWorks database and assign permissions to it.
Equipment Used	For this task, you need access to a machine on which SQL Server is installed.

Objective	To work with Management Studio, roles and permissions.
Criteria for Completion	This task is complete when you log in as your controlled user and experience the control features you have set.

■ PART A: Assigning Permissions to a Role

1. In a query window connected to the AdventureWorks database, execute the following script to create a new role:

```
CREATE ROLE SalesManager AUTHORIZATION dbo;
GO
```

2. This script creates a new database role named SalesManager that is owned by the dbo user.

3. Assign selective permissions to this role for the ProductInventory and JobCandidate tables:

```
GRANT SELECT, INSERT, UPDATE
ON Production.ProductInventory TO SalesManager;
GRANT SELECT
ON HumanResources.JobCandidate TO SalesManager;
```

Any user now assigned to this role will receive Select permissions on the HumanResources.JobCandidate table and Select, Insert, and Update permissions on the Production.ProductInventory table.

Question 1	*You know you can add a user to a role. Can you add a role to a role?*

■ PART B: Testing your Role

1. In Management Studio, add a user (for example, DelaneyUser) to your role.

2. Log off and connect again as the user you added.

3. Try to perform actions both allowed and denied to assure that role permissions meet your expectations.

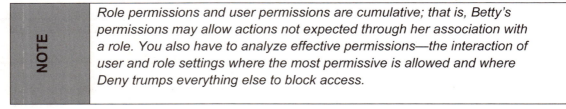

NOTE	*Role permissions and user permissions are cumulative; that is, Betty's permissions may allow actions not expected through her association with a role. You also have to analyze effective permissions—the interaction of user and role settings where the most permissive is allowed and where Deny trumps everything else to block access.*

Exercise 7.2	Changing Execution Context
Scenario	You are a seasoned SQL Server database administrator. You started with SQL Server 6.5 and your company has moved to each new edition. Now you are configuring your applications, stored procedures, and user-defined functions and you wish to avoid chain-of-ownership issues while using schemas effectively. You decide to rewrite many of the software modules to use a standard, fictitious user to whom you assign a really strong password.
Duration	This task should take approximately 15 minutes.
Setup	For this task, you need access to a machine on which SQL Server is installed.
Caveat	You must have administrative privileges on Windows Server.
Procedure	In this exercise, you'll change your execution context to that of another user in the AdventureWorks sample database. You'll use the DelaneyUser user. If you haven't previously created this user, refer to Exercise 6.2. Before running this exercise, revoke the db_datawriter role from this user if you haven't already done so.
Equipment Used	For this task, you need access to a machine on which SQL Server is installed.
Objective	To work with Management Studio and execution contexts.
Criteria for Completion	This task is complete when you have familiarized yourself with the use of execution contexts.

■ PART A: Changing Execution Context

1. Log in to your SQL Server instance as an administrator, and select the **AdventureWorks** database in a new query window.

2. Execute the following:

```
CREATE TABLE ExecutionContext
(systemuser varchar(20), dbuser varchar(20));
GO
INSERT ExecutionContext SELECT SUSER_SNAME(), USER_NAME();
GO
SELECT * FROM ExecutionContext;
```

3. You should see something similar to the following returned:

```
Systemuser    dbuser
-----------   --------------------
SSC10\Steve   Steve
```

4. Execute the following:

```
EXECUTE AS USER = 'DelaneyUser';
GO
SELECT SUSER_SNAME(), USER_NAME();
GO
INSERT ExecutionContext SELECT SUSER_SNAME(), USER_NAME();
GO
SELECT * FROM ExecutionContext;
GO
```

■ PART B: Reviewing Results

1. The first batch changes your execution context from that of a system administrator to that of DelaneyUser, a database user with limited rights. You confirm this change with a simple SELECT statement calling two functions.

2. The third batch attempts to insert data into a new table created by the system administrator. The DelaneyUser shouldn't have rights to this table, and an error should be returned. If you've revoked the db_datareader role rights as well from this user, then the last batch will return an error. Otherwise, it returns the row from the ExecutionContext table.

Exercise 7.3	Encrypting a Column of Data
Scenario	In this exercise, you'll use the AdventureWorks sample database and encrypt two columns of data.
	This exercise will add a column to the HumanResources.EmployeePayHistory table to hold the encrypted values of the Rate column. You'll create an asymmetric key, and then you'll create a symmetric key secured by the asymmetric key. Next, you'll add a column to store the data and encrypt the data, copying it to the new column.
Duration	This task should take approximately 15 minutes.
Setup	For this task, you need access to a machine on which SQL Server is installed.
Caveat	You have created a master key for this database already. If you haven't created this key, refer to Exercise 5.2.
Procedure	In this task, you will work with T-SQL and the query editor to encrypt data.
Equipment Used	For this task, you need access to a machine on which SQL Server is installed.
Objective	To work with cipher schemes in SQL Server.
Criteria for Completion	This task is complete when you examine encrypted data and verify it's unreadable.

■ PART A: Encrypting a Column of Data

1. To create the asymmetric key, type the following into the query editor:

```
CREATE ASYMMETRIC KEY SalaryKey01
WITH ALGORITHM = RSA_1024
ENCRYPTION BY PASSWORD =
'This Key Secures the Symmetric Key';
```

2. Create the symmetric key that will be used to encrypt the data. The asymmetric key created previously is used to secure this key:

```
CREATE SYMMETRIC KEY SalaryKeyEncryptor01
WITH ALGORITHM = DES
ENCRYPTION BY ASYMMETRIC KEY SalaryKey01;
```

3. You need a place to store the encrypted data, so add a column to the table:

```
ALTER TABLE HumanResources.EmployeePayHistory
ADD PayRate varbinary(128);
```

4. You'll use an UPDATE statement to copy the existing rate information into the new column. First, you must open the symmetric key to use it:

```
OPEN SYMMETRIC KEY SalaryKeyEncryptor01
DECRYPTION BY ASYMMETRIC KEY SalaryKey01
WITH PASSWORD = 'This Key Secures the Symmetric Key';
UPDATE HumanResources.EmployeePayHistory
SET PayRate = EncryptByKey(Key_GUID('SalaryKeyEncryptor01')
, CAST(Rate as VARCHAR(10)));
GO
```

5. Select two rows from the table. You should see something similar to the following (note that the ciphertext may be different on your machine):

```
SELECT TOP 2
EmployeeID, Rate, PayRate
, CONVERT(varchar,decryptbykey(PayRate))
as 'Decrypted'
FROM HumanResources.EmployeePayHistory;
```

6. You should see something similar to the following returned:

```
EmployeeID   Rate    PayRate                    Decrypted
----------   ------- ------------------------   ----------
1            12.45   0x00FD57E1DF6E8C439100     12.45
2            13.46   0x00FD57E1DF6E8C439100     13.46
(2 row(s) affected)
```

7. Add another column to the same table to store the data:

```
ALTER TABLE HumanResources.EmployeePayHistory
ADD PayRate2 VARBINARY(512);
```

8. Use an UPDATE statement and the ENCRYPTBYPASSPHRASE( ) function to encrypt the data and store it in the new column:

```
UPDATE HumanResources.EmployeePayHistory
SET PayRate2 = ENCRYPTBYPASSPHRASE
('This is the password',
CAST(Rate AS VARCHAR(20)));
```

■ PART B: Verifying Encryption

1. Verify the encryption by querying the data:

```
SELECT TOP 2
Rate,PayRate2,
CONVERT(VARCHAR(20),
DECRYPTBYPASSPHRASE('This is the password',
PayRate2)) 'Decrypted'
FROM HumanResources.EmployeePayHistory;
```

2. Examine the results:

```
Rate   PayRate2                 Decrypted
12.45  0x0100000040C9BB1FE50A   12.45
13.46  0x0100000068DDA727D0A1   13.46
(2 row(s) affected)
```

Exercise 7.4	Enabling the CLR Environment
Scenario	Your developers want to create some creative database results best programmed in a Visual Studio environment. They ask you to enable CLR so assemblies can be imported.
Duration	This task should take approximately 15 minutes.
Setup	For this task, you need access to a machine on which SQL Server is installed.
Caveat	No special considerations.
Procedure	Use the Query Editor to change configuration.
Equipment Used	For this task, you need access to a machine on which SQL Server is installed. Note that the Surface Area Configuration tool no longer exists in SQL Server 2008.
Objective	To understand server configuration options.
Criteria for Completion	Use the Surface Area Configuration tools check current status and verify results.

■ PART A: Checking the CLR Environment

1. Open the Surface Area Configuration Tool.
2. Click on Surface Area Configuration for Features at the bottom of the dialog box.
3. Open the Database Engine, if necessary, by clicking on the plus symbol.
4. Click on CLR Integration in the tree view.
5. A checkmark in the Enable CLR Integration box indicates the feature is enabled; no checkmark means disabled.

■ PART B: Enabling the CLR Environment

1. Connect to an instance of SQL Server, and open a new query editor window in Management Studio.
2. Type the following in the code window:

```
SP_CONFIGURE 'show advanced options', 1;
GO
RECONFIGURE;
GO
SP_CONFIGURE 'clr enabled', 1;
GO
RECONFIGURE;
GO
```

3. Execute the code by clicking the Execute button. You'll receive a message similar to this one:

```
CONFIGURATION OPTION 'show advanced options'
-- Changed from 0 to 1. Run the RECONFIGURE
-- statement to install.
CONFIGURATION OPTION 'clr enabled'
-- Changed from 0 to 1. Run the RECONFIGURE
-- statement to install.
```

4. Run the following code, and you'll receive a long result set with all the SQL Server options for this instance:

```
SP_CONFIGURE;
```

> **NOTE**
> *One of the result items is named clr enabled. A value of 1 in the run_value column indicates that the CLR is enabled on your instance.*

■ PART C: Verifying Results

1. Return to the Surface Area Configuration Tool to check the resultant status.

LAB 8
DESIGNING A PHYSICAL DATABASE

THIS LAB CONTAINS THE FOLLOWING EXERCISES AND ACTIVITIES:

Exercise 8.1   Generating a Database Schema as a SQL Script

Exercise 8.2   Using Database Diagrams

Exercise 8.3   Modifying Primary Keys

Exercise 8.4   Using the Database Engine Tuning Advisor to Design an Index

Exercise 8.5   Filtering a View

Exercise 8.1	Generating a Database Schema as a SQL Script
Scenario	You are preparing your Business Recovery Plan. You suddenly realize all objects have been created in the Management Studio GUI. You don't want to re-create them manually—besides you don't remember everything you did. You decide to script all objects and save the resultant files offsite in a secure place.
Duration	This task should take approximately 15 minutes.
Setup	For this task, you need access to a machine on which SQL Server is installed.
Caveat	You must have administrative privileges on SQL Server.
Procedure	In this exercise, you'll use Management Studio to reproduce scripts for all objects.
Equipment Used	For this task, you need access to a machine on which SQL Server is installed.

Objective	To understand how to create a database script.
Criteria for Completion	This task is complete when you re-create a few objects in the second instance on your server.

■ PART A: Generating a Database Schema as a SQL Script

1. From the Start menu, select **All Programs** then **Microsoft SQL Server** then **SQL Server Management Studio**.

2. In Object Explorer, connect to a SQL Server Database Engine instance, and then expand that instance.

3. Expand **Databases**, and then right click the **AdventureWorks** database.

4. Select **Script Database As** from the context menu, and then select **Create To** from the next context menu.

5. The next context menu gives you the choice of creating the script in a New Query Editor window, writing to a file, or saving to the Clipboard. You'll most commonly save the script to a file; but in this example, send it to a New Query Editor Window so that you can change it and run the resulting script.

> **NOTE**
> *You can use the process shown to generate scripts for any part of the database, such as tables, views, and so on. You can generate scripts from the objects in an existing database and then add these objects to another database by running the scripts against that database. In effect, this re-creates the complete database structure and any individual database objects.*

■ PART B: Verifying Success

1. Review the SQL commands in the query window. Notice what was automatically scripted for you (Figure 8-1).

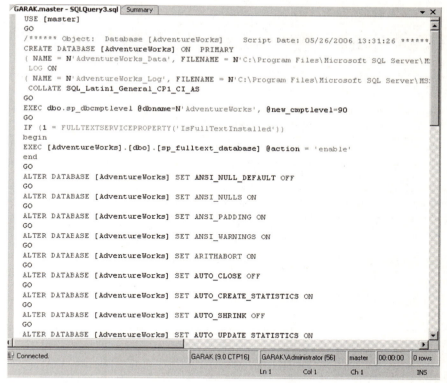

```
GARAK.master - SQLQuery3.sql   Summary                                              ▾ ×
    USE [master]
    GO
    /****** Object:  Database [AdventureWorks]      Script Date: 05/26/2006 13:31:26 ******
    CREATE DATABASE [AdventureWorks] ON  PRIMARY
    ( NAME = N'AdventureWorks_Data', FILENAME = N'C:\Program Files\Microsoft SQL Server\M:
     LOG ON
    ( NAME = N'AdventureWorks_Log', FILENAME = N'C:\Program Files\Microsoft SQL Server\MS:
     COLLATE SQL_Latin1_General_CP1_CI_AS
    GO
    EXEC dbo.sp_dbcmptlevel @dbname=N'AdventureWorks', @new_cmptlevel=90
    GO
    IF (1 = FULLTEXTSERVICEPROPERTY('IsFullTextInstalled'))
    begin
    EXEC [AdventureWorks].[dbo].[sp_fulltext_database] @action = 'enable'
    end
    GO
    ALTER DATABASE [AdventureWorks] SET ANSI_NULL_DEFAULT OFF
    GO
    ALTER DATABASE [AdventureWorks] SET ANSI_NULLS ON
    GO
    ALTER DATABASE [AdventureWorks] SET ANSI_PADDING ON
    GO
    ALTER DATAEASE [AdventureWorks] SET ANSI_WARNINGS ON
    GO
    ALTER DATAEASE [AdventureWorks] SET ARITHABORT ON
    GO
    ALTER DATABASE [AdventureWorks] SET AUTO_CLOSE OFF
    GO
    ALTER DATABASE [AdventureWorks] SET AUTO_CREATE_STATISTICS ON
    GO
    ALTER DATABASE [AdventureWorks] SET AUTO_SHRINK OFF
    GO
    ALTER DATABASE [AdventureWorks] SET AUTO_UPDATE_STATISTICS ON
Connected.                          GARAK (9.0 CTP16)   GARAK\Administrator (56)   master   00:00:00   0 rows
                                    Ln 1          Col 1          Ch 1              INS
```

Figure 8-1
Query Editor Window from 'Script Database As' Selection

2. From the Management Studio menu, select **Edit**, then select **Find and Replace**, then click on **Quick Replace**. In the 'Find what' box, enter **Adventure**. In the 'Replace with' box, enter **Clone**. Next click on the **Replace All** button. This will change all occurrences of 'Adventure' to 'Clone' in the current query window command script. Click on **OK** when the change completes and then close the Find and Replace window.

3. Click on **Execute** to run the revised query. Wait for the query to complete.

4. Right click on **Databases** in the Object Explorer panel. Select and click on **Refresh** to refresh the list of databases. Notice the new CloneWorks database. You have just created this database from the script. The name was changed in step 2. Note that only the basic database was created. Tables and other objects can be scripted the same way.

> **NOTE**
> *If you did not change the names or ran the script twice on the same instance, the script will fail because the names already exist. You cannot have two databases with the same name in the same instance nor can you have the same Windows filename used for more than one database on the same server.*

Exercise 8.2	Using Database Diagrams
Scenario	At a database conference, the speaker said you could completely manage a database from a database diagram. You came home. Now you want to try it. Is it true?
Duration	This task should take approximately 15 minutes.
Setup	For this task, you need access to a machine on which SQL Server is installed.
Caveat	You must have administrative privileges on Windows Server.
Procedure	Create a database diagram for AdventureWorks and for administrative tools.
Equipment Used	For this task, you need access to a machine on which SQL Server is installed.
Objective	To work with database diagrams.
Criteria for Completion	This task is complete when you have familiarized yourself with database diagrams and their capabilities.

■ PART A: Using Database Diagrams

1. From the Start menu, select **All Programs** then **Microsoft SQL Server** then **SQL Server Management Studio**.

2. In Object Explorer, connect to a SQL Server Database Engine instance, and then expand that instance.

3. Expand **Databases**, and then expand the **AdventureWorks** database.

4. Right click **Database Diagrams** under the AdventureWorks Sales database, and click **New Database Diagram**.

 You may have to approve additonal setup steps. You may get a message stating "This database does not have one or more of the support objects required to use database diagramming. Do you wish to create them? Reply "Yes."

5. In the Add Table dialog, select **Contact (Person)**, **ContactCreditCard (Sales)**, and **Credit Card (Sales)**, and click **Add**.

6. After the tables have been added, click **Close**, and you'll see your database diagram. Notice the two foreign-key relationships as shown in Figure 8-2.

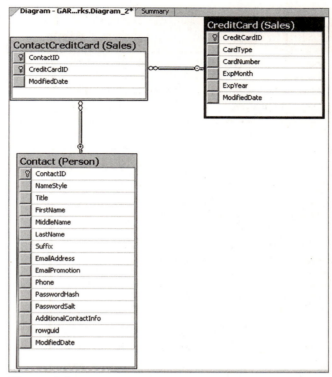

Figure 8-2
Database Diagram with Foreign Keys

■ PART B: Verifying Results

1. Right click the blank space inside a table box. Examine the options that you have available.
2. Right click the blank space outside a table box. Again, look at your context menu choices.
3. Try displaying data or creating a table or adding an index.

Exercise 8.3	Modifying Primary Keys
Scenario	United States Social Security numbers are supposed to be unique but errors occur. This can present a problem if the number is used as a primary key and alleged duplicates occur. As a temporary solution, you have decided to add a column and use a surrogate value to maintain uniqueness.
Duration	This task should take approximately 15 minutes.
Setup	For this task, you need access to a machine on which SQL Server is installed.
Caveat	You must have administrative privileges on Windows Server.
Procedure	In this task, you will work with Management Studio and table objects.

Equipment Used	For this task, you need access to a machine on which SQL Server is installed.
Objective	To work with Windows System Monitor.
Criteria for Completion	This task is complete when you have familiarized yourself with modifying table properties.

■ PART A: Modifying Primary Keys

1. Open Management Studio by selecting it from the SQL Server group in Programs on your Start menu, and connect using Windows Authentication.
2. In Object Explorer, expand **Databases** then **AdventureWorks** then **Tables**.
3. Right click the **Person.Contact** table, and select **Modify**.

> **NOTE**
> *If you have applied current service packs, the Modify is gone—try Design.*

4. In the Table Designer screen (Figure 8-3), notice that just to the left of the ContactID field is a small key icon, denoting that this is the primary key.

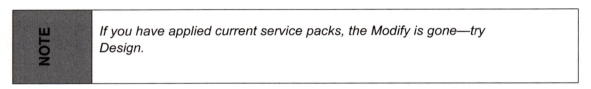

Table - Person.Contact	Summary	
Column Name	**Data Type**	**Allow Nulls**
ContactID	int	☐
NameStyle	NameStyle:bit	☐
Title	nvarchar(8)	☑
FirstName	Name:nvarchar(50)	☐
MiddleName	Name:nvarchar(50)	☑
LastName	Name:nvarchar(50)	☐
Suffix	nvarchar(10)	☑
EmailAddress	nvarchar(50)	☑
EmailPromotion	int	☐
Phone	Phone:nvarchar(...	☑
PasswordHash	varchar(40)	☐
PasswordSalt	varchar(10)	☐
AdditionalContactInfo	xml(CONTENT Pe...	☑
rowguid	uniqueidentifier	☐
ModifiedDate	datetime	☐
		☐

Figure 8-3
Table Designer Screen

5. Right click the **Title** column name, and notice that you can set this column as the primary key. But instead:

    * Insert a new column, call it **RowID** with an int datatype

    * Look at the column properties near the bottom of the screen and change **Is Identity** to **Yes**

    * Right click your new **RowID** and choose **Set Primary Key**.

NOTE	*You will get a warning that a primary key already exists. Go ahead and acknowledge that you do, indeed, want to make RowID the new primary. This will take a moment as SQL Server must delete the existing index on ContactID, drop the existing column, and create a new index on RowID before you can continue.*

6. You now have a surrogate key. Close the **Table Designer**.

Question 1	*In Table Designer, how do you make ContactID and RowID a composite key?*

Exercise 8.4	Using the Database Engine Tuning Advisor to Design an Index
Scenario	You have just installed new queries requested by the financial analysts. They expect to use the new routines and ignore the old ones. You're an experienced database administrator so you leave the old ones in place, anyway. Who knows?
	You do know current statistics will be all out of whack. You decide to create a workload file over the course of the next week to capture actual query usage. Then you plan to use the workload in the Database Tuning Wizard and implement its suggestions.
	And then, do it all over again the following week.
Duration	This task should take approximately 15 minutes.
Setup	For this task, you need access to a machine on which SQL Server is installed.
Caveat	You must have appropriate privileges on SQL Server.
Procedure	In this task, you will create a workload and use the Database Tuning Wizard.
Equipment Used	For this task, you need access to a machine on which SQL Server is installed.
Objective	To work with Database Tuning Wizard.
Criteria for Completion	This task is complete when you have finished evaluating the Database Tuning Wizard's suggestions and examined the reports.

■ PART A: Using the Database Engine Tuning Advisor to Design an Index

1. Open SQL Server Profiler by choosing **Start** then **All Programs** then **Microsoft SQL Server** then **Performance Tools** then **SQL Server Profiler**.

2. Choose **File** then **New Trace**. This brings up the Trace Properties dialog box. Connect to SQL Server when prompted.

3. For the Trace Name, enter **AWIndexTrace** as shown in Figure 8-4.

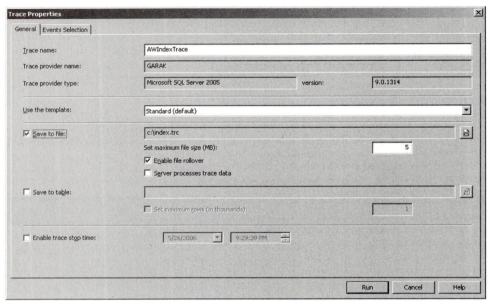

Figure 8-4
Trace Properties Dialog Box

4. Select the **Save to file** check box.

5. In the Save to file dialog box, enter **C:\index.trc**, and click Save.

6. Click **Run** on the Trace Properties dialog box to start the trace.

7. From the Tools menu, select **Management Studio**, and connect using Windows Authentication.

8. Click the **New Query** button on the toolbar, and select **New SQL Server Query**. Connect with Windows Authentication if requested.

9. Enter the following code in the query window:

```
USE AdventureWorks;

SELECT * FROM Person.Contact;
```

10. Execute the query by clicking the **Execute** button on the toolbar.

11. Delete the previous query, and enter and execute another query to generate a little more traffic:

```
USE AdventureWorks;

SELECT * FROM Sales.SalesOrderDetail;
```

12. Switch back to Profiler, and stop the trace by clicking the **red button** just above the TextData window (see Figure 8-5). Notice that the queries you just executed are listed in the trace (there may be quite a bit of information from the system services as well as the SQL Server Agent).

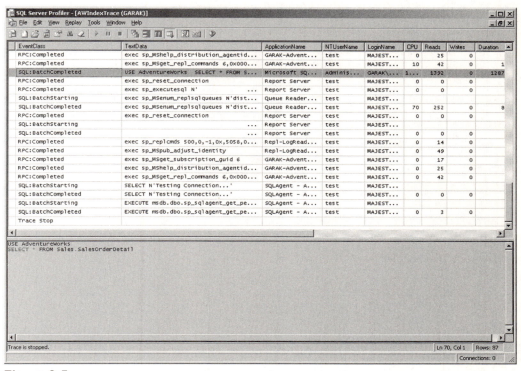

Figure 8-5
SQL Server Profiler Trace Contents

13. Open the **Database Engine Tuning Advisor** from the **Microsoft SQL Server** then **Performance Tools** program group on the Start menu, and connect using Windows Authentication. A new session is created for you.

14. Make sure the General tab is selected, and enter AdventureWorksIndex Session in the Session name box. Notice that the session name in the Session Monitor on the left is changed for you as you type.

15. In the Workload section, leave the File radio button selected, and enter **C:\index.trc** in the filename text box.

16. In the Databases and tables to tune grid, check the box next to **AdventureWorks**.

17. In the Selected Tables column, click the **down arrow** or the hyperlink to see all the tables that are selected (Figure 8-6).

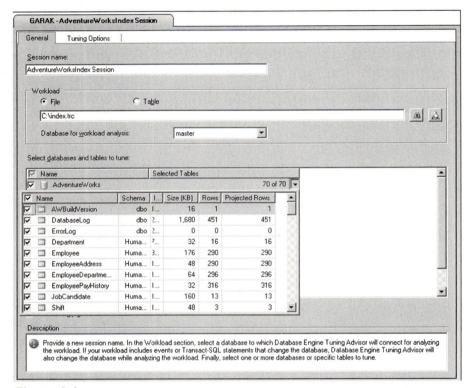

Figure 8-6
Database Engine Tuning Advisor—General Tab

18. Switch to the **Tuning Options** tab (Figure 8-7), and note the default settings. Make sure the Partitioning strategy to employ is set to No partitioning.

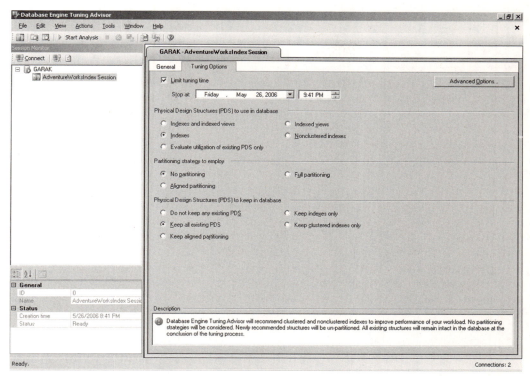

Figure 8-7
Database Engine Tuning Advisor—Tuning Options Tab

19. Click the **Advanced Options** button, and note—but don't change—the settings shown in
Figure 8-8.

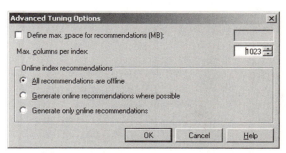

Figure 8-8
Advanced Tuning Options Dialog Box

20. Click **Cancel** to return to the Tuning Options tab.

21. Switch back to the **General** tab.

22. On the Actions menu, click **Start Analysis**, and click **OK** on the Start Analysis dialog box.
Tuning Progress will be shown on the **Progress** tab (Figure 8-9).

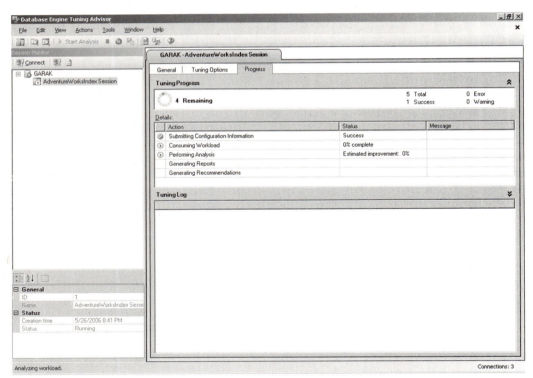

Figure 8-9
Database Engine Tuning Advisor—Progress Tab

23. When the analysis is complete, you'll be given a list of recommendations (there are no valid recommendations shown in Figure 8-10 because the sample database is already tuned).

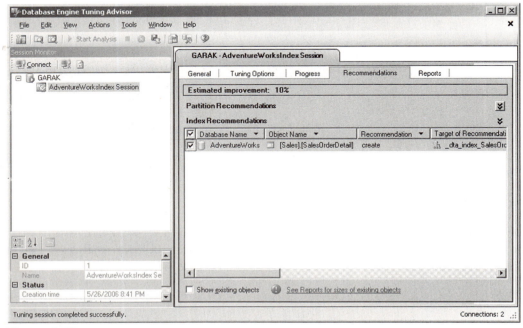

Figure 8-10
Database Engine Tuning Advisor—Recommendations Tab

24. Switch to the **Reports** tab (Figure 8-11), and select a report from the **Select report** drop-down list to see reports of tuning and database statistics.

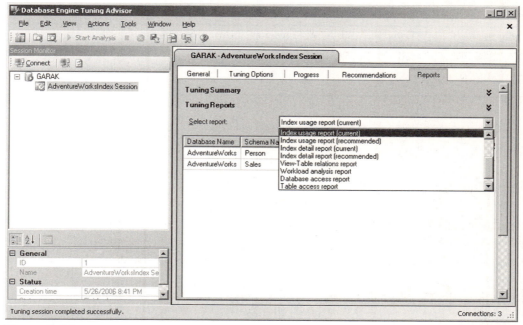

Figure 8-11
Database Engine Tuning Advisor—Reports Tab

This method, although it may seem a bit time consuming, can save you a great deal of effort. Because most of the work while creating an index is in deciding the columns on which to create the index, you can save yourself aggravation and reduce errors by letting the Database Engine Tuning Advisor decide for you. Bear in mind that this method isn't foolproof, so always verify it.

Exercise 8.5	Filtering a View
Scenario	The Director of Human Resources is tired of publishing a building telephone directory. She comes to you. Can you help?
	Why not create a view against the Human Resources Personnel table to display the last name, first name, and telephone number of all employees? You then ask your crack developer to make a little application that shows an icon on everyone's desktop that when opened, allows users to enter the first few letters of the last name (enough to be unique) and the first few letters of a first name and return a telephone number.
	You're a hero!
Duration	This task should take approximately 15 minutes.
Setup	For this task, you need access to a machine on which SQL Server is installed.
Caveat	You must have administrative privileges on SQL Server.

Procedure	In this task, you will work with Management Studio to create a view.
Equipment Used	For this task, you need access to a machine on which SQL Server is installed.
Objective	To work with Management Studio and views.
Criteria for Completion	This task is complete when you have successfully built a new filtered view.

■ PART A: Filtering a View

1. Open Management Studio by choosing **Start** then **All Programs** then **Microsoft SQL Server** then **SQL Server Management Studio**.
2. In Object Explorer, connect to a SQL Server Database Engine instance, and then expand that instance.
3. Expand **Databases**, and then expand the **AdventureWorks** database. Expand the **Views** folder.
4. Right click the **HumanResources.vEmployeeDepartment** view. Click **Open View**. The view returns a table of data, as shown in Figure 8-12.

EmployeeID	Title	FirstName	MiddleName	LastName	Suffix	JobTitle
15	NULL	Jeffrey	L	Ford	NULL	Production Tec
16	NULL	Jo	A	Brown	NULL	Production Sup
17	NULL	Doris	M	Hartwig	NULL	Production Tec
18	NULL	John	T	Campbell	NULL	Production Sup
19	NULL	Diane	R	Glimp	NULL	Production Tec
20	NULL	Steven	T	Selikoff	NULL	Production Tec
21	NULL	Peter	J	Krebs	NULL	Production Cor
22	NULL	Stuart	V	Munson	NULL	Production Tec
23	NULL	Greg	F	Alderson	NULL	Production Tec
24	NULL	David	N	Johnson	NULL	Production Tec
25	NULL	Zheng	W	Mu	NULL	Production Sup
26	NULL	Ivo	William	Salmre	NULL	Production Tec
27	NULL	Paul	B	Komosinski	NULL	Production Tec
28	NULL	Ashvini	R	Sharma	NULL	Network Admin
29	NULL	Kendall	C	Keil	NULL	Production Tec
30	NULL	Paula	M	Barreto de Mattos	NULL	Human Resour
31	NULL	Alejandro	E	McGuel	NULL	Production Tec
32	NULL	Garrett	R	Young	NULL	Production Tec
33	NULL	Jian Shuo	NULL	Wang	NULL	Production Tec
34	NULL	Susan	W	Eaton	NULL	Stocker
35	NULL	Vamsi	N	Kuppa	NULL	Shipping and R
36	NULL	Alice	O	Ciccu	NULL	Production Tec
37	NULL	Simon	D	Rapier	NULL	Production Tec
38	NULL	Jinghao	K	Liu	NULL	Production Sup
39	NULL	Michael	T	Hines	NULL	Production Tec
40	NULL	Yvonne	S	McKay	NULL	Production Tec

Figure 8-12
Example View

5. Suppose all you want is a subset of the data—for example, only the employees assigned to the Production Department. You can create another view, or you can filter the current view. To do so, right click the **HumanResources.vEmployeeDepartment view**, and select **Modify** from the context menu.

<table>
<tr>
<td>**NOTE**</td>
<td>*If you have applied recent service packs, Modify is gone—try Design.*</td>
</tr>
</table>

6. You're now presented with a graphical image of related tables (Figure 8-13); a table showing columns that form the view; and some information such as aliases, the table the column is from, sort type, and so on. Note the Filter table column. Below it is a pane with the T-SQL commands that define the HumanResources.vEmployeeDepartment view. The final pane is currently blank.

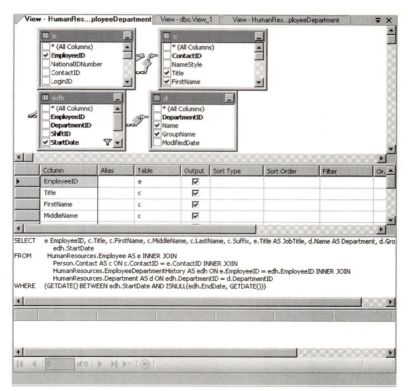

Figure 8-13
Modifying a View

7. Scroll down until you locate the Name column as shown in Figure 8-14. Note that it has an Alias of Department. Under Filter, enter **Production**. As soon as you leave the cell, the editor edits your entry to the correct code and adds the new filter to the original T-SQL WHERE statement.

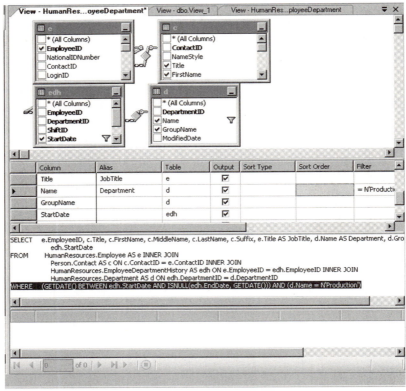

Figure 8-14
Modifying a View—After Modification

8. Execute your query to test whether your filter worked. The resulting output in the lowermost pane shows the effects of the filter. In the new table, you should see only employees whose department is Production (see Figure 8-15).

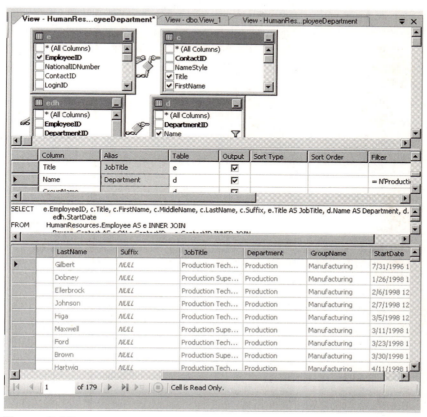

Figure 8-15
Modified View with Filtered Results

9. To make your change permanent, save the modified view. Once the changes are saved, the filter will be applied whenever you open the view as shown in Figure 8-16.

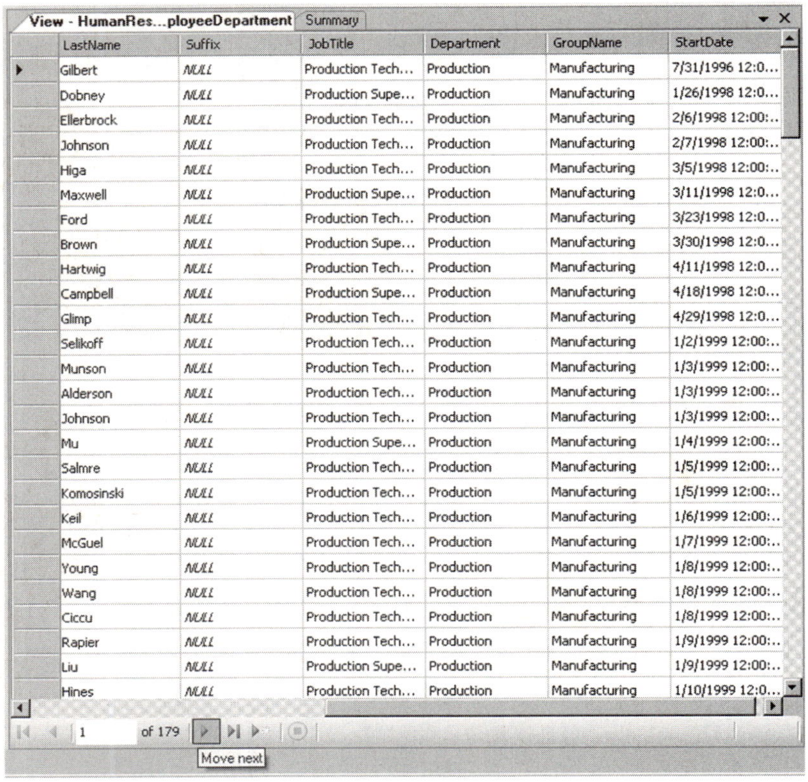

LastName	Suffix	JobTitle	Department	GroupName	StartDate
Gilbert	NULL	Production Tech...	Production	Manufacturing	7/31/1996 12:0...
Dobney	NULL	Production Supe...	Production	Manufacturing	1/26/1998 12:0...
Ellerbrock	NULL	Production Tech...	Production	Manufacturing	2/6/1998 12:00:...
Johnson	NULL	Production Tech...	Production	Manufacturing	2/7/1998 12:00:...
Higa	NULL	Production Tech...	Production	Manufacturing	3/5/1998 12:00:...
Maxwell	NULL	Production Supe...	Production	Manufacturing	3/11/1998 12:0...
Ford	NULL	Production Tech...	Production	Manufacturing	3/23/1998 12:0...
Brown	NULL	Production Supe...	Production	Manufacturing	3/30/1998 12:0...
Hartwig	NULL	Production Tech...	Production	Manufacturing	4/11/1998 12:0...
Campbell	NULL	Production Supe...	Production	Manufacturing	4/18/1998 12:0...
Glimp	NULL	Production Tech...	Production	Manufacturing	4/29/1998 12:0...
Selikoff	NULL	Production Tech...	Production	Manufacturing	1/2/1999 12:00:...
Munson	NULL	Production Tech...	Production	Manufacturing	1/3/1999 12:00:...
Alderson	NULL	Production Tech...	Production	Manufacturing	1/3/1999 12:00:...
Johnson	NULL	Production Tech...	Production	Manufacturing	1/3/1999 12:00:...
Mu	NULL	Production Supe...	Production	Manufacturing	1/4/1999 12:00:...
Salmre	NULL	Production Tech...	Production	Manufacturing	1/5/1999 12:00:...
Komosinski	NULL	Production Tech...	Production	Manufacturing	1/5/1999 12:00:...
Keil	NULL	Production Tech...	Production	Manufacturing	1/6/1999 12:00:...
McGuel	NULL	Production Tech...	Production	Manufacturing	1/7/1999 12:00:...
Young	NULL	Production Tech...	Production	Manufacturing	1/8/1999 12:00:...
Wang	NULL	Production Tech...	Production	Manufacturing	1/8/1999 12:00:...
Ciccu	NULL	Production Tech...	Production	Manufacturing	1/8/1999 12:00:...
Rapier	NULL	Production Tech...	Production	Manufacturing	1/9/1999 12:00:...
Liu	NULL	Production Supe...	Production	Manufacturing	1/9/1999 12:00:...
Hines	NULL	Production Tech...	Production	Manufacturing	1/10/1999 12:0...

View - HumanRes...ployeeDepartment | Summary

1 of 179 ▶ ▶| ▶

Move next

Figure 8-16
Example View After Filtering

LAB 9
CREATING DATABASE CONVENTIONS AND STANDARDS

THIS LAB CONTAINS THE FOLLOWING EXERCISES AND ACTIVITIES:

Exercise 9.1   Evaluating Object Names in AdventureWorks

Exercise 9.2   Using Template Explorer

Exercise 9.1	Evaluating Object Names in AdventureWorks
Scenario	Your developers are yelling at you; your analysts are yelling at you; you're frustrated, too, all because everyone's having troubles understanding the data as they each perform their own tasks.
	You decide to sit everyone down to agree on meaningful naming standards.
Duration	This task should take approximately 30 minutes.
Setup	For this task, you need access to a machine on which SQL Server is installed.
Caveat	You must have administrative privileges on Windows Server.
Procedure	In this exercise, you'll examine the AdventureWorks database.
Equipment Used	For this task, you need access to a machine on which SQL Server is installed.
Objective	To appreciate the value of consistent naming schemes.
Criteria for Completion	This task is complete when you have familiarized yourself with the options available to you.

■ PART A: Evaluating Object Names in AdventureWorks

1. Open **SQL Server Management Studio**.
2. In the Connect To Server dialog box, connect to an instance where you've installed the AdventureWorks database.
3. In Object Explorer, in the Databases folder, expand the **AdventureWorks** database.
4. Use Object Explorer to examine the names of objects in the Tables, Views, and Programmability folders.
5. To view columns, keys, constraints, triggers, and indexes, expand each table in the Tables folder.
6. Close **SQL Server Management Studio** when you've finished.
7. Determine whether the following items exist, and provide an example.

   From any database object:
   - Provide a proper use of uppercase and lowercase names.
   - Is an object named with a prefix (if appropriate)?

   Tables:
   - Are singular table names used?
   - Do table names correspond to the names of entities or relations?

   Views:
   - Do views come with a standard prefix? What is it?
   - Does the name reflect the purpose of the view?

   Stored procedures:
   - Do the user-stored procedures use a standard prefix?
   - Do system-stored procedures use the same prefix?

   Functions:
   - Do user-defined functions have a standard prefix?
   - Does the function name begin with a verb?
   - Explain why dbo.ufnLeadingZeros is either a good or badly named function.

   Triggers:
   - Do Data Modification Language (DML) triggers use a prefix that reflects the events they apply to?
   - Do DML triggers include the name of the table they belong to?
   - There is only one Data Definition Language (DDL) trigger; does it indicate the type of operation being performed?

   Indexes:
   - Do indexes include a prefix that indicates their type?
   - Do indexes always include the name of the original table?
   - Do indexes include the names of the columns in the index?
   - Are the names of objects and columns separated by an underscore?

Constraints:

- Do constraints include a prefix that indicates their type, such as CK or DF?
- Do the constraints include the name of the original table and the names of the columns involved?

8. Schemas in the AdventureWorks database don't follow good naming conventions. Provide examples of the following, and explain why they might be considered bad practices:

- Schemas don't include prefixes designating them as schema.
- Some schemas use singular names, whereas others use plural names.

Exercise 9.2	Using Template Explorer
Scenario	You are experiencing difficulties in troubleshooting long-running queries. You've discovered each developer writes code in a unique style. You decide to have a meeting to enforce standard approaches. Everyone eventually agrees to start by writing templates that everyone can and will use.
Duration	This task should take approximately 15 minutes.
Setup	For this task, you need access to a machine on which SQL Server is installed.
Caveat	For readability and consistency, try using templates for T-SQL code.
Procedure	In this task, you will work with Template Explorer.
Equipment Used	For this task, you need access to a machine on which SQL Server is installed.
Objective	To work with Template Explorer.
Criteria for Completion	This task is complete when you have familiarized yourself with Template Explorer.

■ PART A: Using Template Explorer

1. Open **SQL Server Management Studio**.
2. Click **View**, and select **Template Explorer**.
3. In the Template Explorer Pane (on the right side of your screen), select the **Stored Procedure** folder, and expand it.
4. Double click the file **Create Procedure Basic Template**. If prompted, log in to the database engine.

5. The template opens in a Query Explorer window, as shown in Figure 9-1.

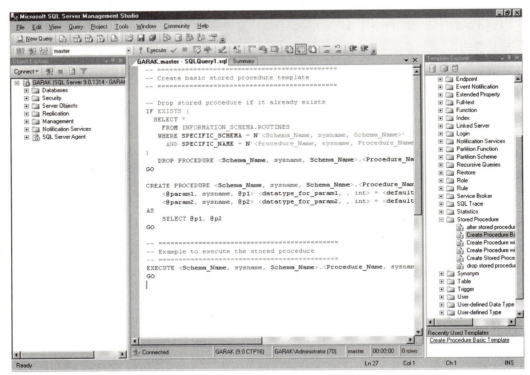

Figure 9-1
SQL Server Management Studio Showing Template Explorer and an Example Template

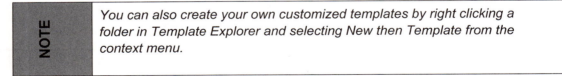

> **NOTE**
> *You can also create your own customized templates by right clicking a folder in Template Explorer and selecting New then Template from the context menu.*

6. Examine the template script, and note the various components.
7. Repeat these steps for a number of other commonly created objects.

LAB 10
DESIGNING A SQL SERVER SOLUTION FOR HIGH AVAILABILITY

THIS LAB CONTAINS THE FOLLOWING EXERCISES AND ACTIVITIES:

Exercise 10.1   Setting Up Database Mirroring

Exercise 10.2   Designing RAID Arrays

Exercise 10.1	Setting Up Database Mirroring
Scenario	You're examining your Business Recovery Plan, again. This time you ask yourself: "What if this building burns down?" In your case, you have a buried fiber optic cable to the next building. Why not create a complete duplicate of the database next door?
Duration	This task should take approximately 30 minutes.
Setup	For this task, you need access to a second installed instance of SQL Server.
Caveat	You must have a named instance installed.
Procedure	Use the Database Mirroring Security Wizard to establish a mirror between your default instance and one of your named instances.
Equipment Used	Conceptually, two independent SQL Server installations and a witness server.
Objective	To understand database mirroring

Criteria for Completion	This task is complete when you make a change on the primary instance and find it mirrored to the secondary instance.

■ PART A: Setting Up Database Mirroring

1. After connecting to your first SQL Server server, open a query editor instance, and execute the following to perform a full backup of AdventureWorks:

```
BACKUP DATABASE AdventureWorks
TO DISK = 'C:\program files\Microsoft SQL
Server\mssql.1\mssql\backup\adventure.bak';
```

> **NOTE**
> *The default instance is in the file path . . . \mssql.1\ . . . Other instances are in the order as installed; (e.g., Analysis Services could be . . . \mssql.2\ . . .). Look in the file path of your installation. OLTP instances have a directory structure just like the default instance. Everything else has a different look.*

2. Restore this backup as AdventureWorks on the second instance of SQL Server. Doing so initializes the mirror database:

```
RESTORE DATABASE AdventureWorks
FROM DISK =
'C:\Program Files\Microsoft SQL Server
\MSSQL.1\MSSQL\Backup\Adventure.bak'
WITH MOVE 'AdventureWorks_Data' TO
'C:\Program Files\Microsoft SQL Server
\MSSQL.2\MSSQL\Data\AdventureWorksMirror_Data.mdf'
, MOVE 'AdventureWorks_Log' TO
'C:\Program Files\Microsoft SQL Server
\MSSQL.2\MSSQL\Data\AdventureWorksMirror_Log.ldf'
, NORECOVERY;
```

3. After the restore is complete, you can begin mirroring. Right click the **AdventureWorks** database on the first instance in Management Studio, and select **Tasks** and then **Mirror**, as shown in Figure 10-1, which opens the mirroring database properties (Figure 10-2).

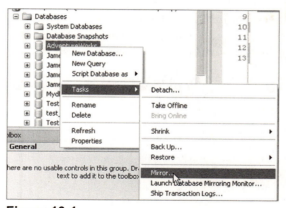

Figure 10-1
A Portion of Management Studio Showing the Tasks and Mirror
Selections

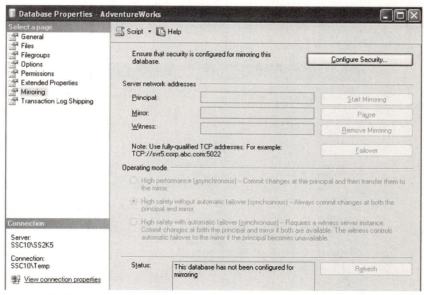

Figure 10-2
Database Properties—Mirroring

4. Click the **Configure Security** button to start the Database Mirroring Security Wizard. After the welcome screen, the next screen offers the choice of implementing a witness server. As shown in Figure 10-3, in this exercise you won't use a witness server.

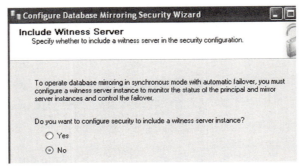

Figure 10-3
Configure Database Mirroring Security Wizard

5. The next screen is a configuration screen. After clicking **Next**, you'll see the principal server endpoint configuration (Figure 10-4).

Figure 10-4
Mirroring Wizard—Principal Server Instance

Question 1	How many mirroring sessions may you have per database? Per server?

6. Click **Next** to reach the mirror server endpoint configuration (Figure 10-5). Click **Connect** and connect to the second instance. Accept the defaults for ports and endpoint names by clicking **Next**.

Figure 10-5
Mirroring Wizard—Mirror Server Instance

7. The service account page appears (Figure 10-6). In this case, you have set the accounts to match the instance on which mirroring is set up.

Figure 10-6
Mirroring Wizard—Service Accounts

8. After clicking Next, everything is now configured, and a confirmation screen similar to the one shown in Figure 10-7 appears. Click **Finish**, and the endpoints will be created.

Figure 10-7
Configure Database Mirroring Security Wizard—Completion

9. The last screen that appears (Figure 10-8) lets you start mirroring. Click **Start Mirroring** to enable mirroring between these two databases.

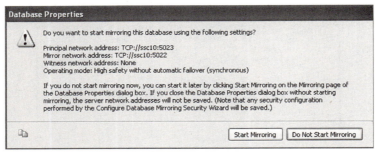

Figure 10-8
Start Mirroring Option Window

NOTE

You must install service packs individually to each instance. If you have not applied updates to your instance you must start the SQL Server server service for that instance with the Trace Flag 1400 enabled.

■ PART B: Verify Success

1. Add data to a known location in AdventureWorks on the principal server.
2. Connect to the instance you used and verify the changes are there. Allow for propagation time.

Exercise 10.2	Designing RAID Arrays
Scenario	In this exercise, you'll examine potentially building a series of RAID arrays for an instance of SQL Server. The decision has been made to build one 20+ GB array for the OS and page files, one 70+ GB array for the log files, one 500+ GB array for the data files, and one 50+ GB array for the tempdb database. You have many 35 GB and 70 GB drives available for the arrays. Your server can hold a maximum of 18 drives. This may limit your design.
Duration	This task should take approximately 15 minutes.
Setup	There are no configuration requirements.
Caveat	This task doesn't have any caveats.
Procedure	This is a paper and pencil exercise. Examine the described infrastructure of the scenario and choose one or more RAID solutions. Be sure to consider the performance costs of RAID as well as the various RAID types and the maximum number of drives possible on the server.
Equipment Used	There are no equipment requirements.
Objective	To think through and solve a real-world situation involving server and RAID configuration choices.
Criteria for Completion	This task is complete when you have familiarized yourself with RAID options and planned out a workable drive layout.

■ PART A: Designing RAID Arrays

1. Draw out a diagram of the server showing 18 drive locations.
2. Consider the scenario. How would you configure this system?
3. Label each drive location on your diagram with the drive size and identify which array the drive belongs to.
4. If you had 146 GB drives available, how would your design change?

Complete this exercise on your own before referring to the explanation that follows. If you disagree with the recommended solution, explain why.

Possible Recommendations/Explanations

1. The first array for the OS and page file has minimal read and write activity. A RAID 1 array is most appropriate for this purpose. Because the data size isn't large, two drives in a mirror will probably be enough for this array. You can support this with two 35 GB drives, so you should choose this size.

2. The second array will support the log files for the databases. Because log files are primarily write-only files, use a RAID 10 array for these files. You need 70 GB drives, but to gain the benefits of multiple spindles, choose four 35 GB drives rather than two 70 GB drives in a RAID 1 configuration.

3. The third array is for the data files. A RAID 5 array is a good choice here unless the transactional activity is very high. In that case, you should choose a RAID 10 array with enough drives to give the space needed and as many spindles as possible. Because this is a large array, choose nine 70 GB drives, giving 560 GB of usable space (8 × 70 GB) with 70 GB devoted to parity information.

4. The last array is for tempdb. Again depending on the performance needed, you may want to choose a RAID 5 array or RAID 10 array. Perhaps the limit on the number of drives will influence your decision. A two 70 GB RAID 1 array will suffice.

5. Upgrading to higher capacity drives can reduce the number of drives required for the data array; however for the other arrays, drive capacity is not an issue.

LAB 11
DESIGNING A DATA RECOVERY SOLUTION FOR A DATABASE

Exercise 11.1	Creating a Backup Device
Scenario	You've been reviewing your Disaster Recovery Plan. The cornerstone of this plan is to perform regular backups and store the results somewhere else. You start by checking your backup devices. Do they still perform as intended?
Duration	This task should take approximately 15 minutes.
Setup	For this task, you need access to a machine on which SQL Server is installed.
Caveat	You must have administrative privileges on SQL Server.

Procedure	Check for existing devices and check their properties. Then create a new backup device.
Equipment Used	For this task, you need access to a machine on which SQL Server is installed.
Objective	To examine and create backup devices.
Criteria for Completion	This task is complete when you have your new backup device listed in Management Studio.

■ PART A: Creating a Backup Device

1. Open **SQL Server Management Studio** by selecting it from the SQL Server group under Programs on the Start menu. Expand your server, and then expand the **Server Objects** folder.

2. Click on **Backup Devices**. Are any listed? If yes, right click on one to examine its configuration.

3. In either case, now right click **Backup Device** and select **New Backup Device** from the context menu.

4. In the Device name box of the Backup Device dialog box (Figure 11-1), enter **AdvWorksFull**. Notice that the filename and path are filled in for you; make sure you have enough free space on the drive that SQL Server has selected; or select your own location.

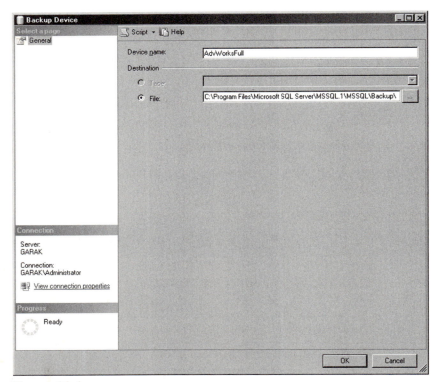

Figure 11-1
Backup Device Dialog Box

5. Click **OK** to create the device.

> | | |
> |---|---|
> | **NOTE** | *If you use a tape drive as a backup device, it must be physically attached to the SQL Server machine.* |

Exercise 11.2	Performing a Full Backup with Management Studio
Scenario	Continuing with your review of your Disaster Recovery Plan, you have revised your thoughts about how often a full backup should be performed. You need to create additional jobs to meet these new needs.
Duration	This task should take approximately 15 minutes.
Setup	For this task, you need access to a machine on which SQL Server is installed.
Caveat	You must have administrative privileges on SQL Server.
Procedure	In this task, you will use Management Studio to manually perform a backup.
Equipment Used	For this task, you need access to a machine on which SQL Server is installed.
Objective	To understand backup configuration options.
Criteria for Completion	This task is complete when the restore utility locates and displays your backup.

■ PART A: Performing a Full Backup with Management Studio

1. Open **Management Studio**. Expand your server and then expand **Databases**.
2. Right click **AdventureWorks**, and select **Properties**.

3. On the Options page (Figure 11-2), change the **Recovery model** from Simple to **Full** using the drop-down box so that you can perform a transaction log backup later.

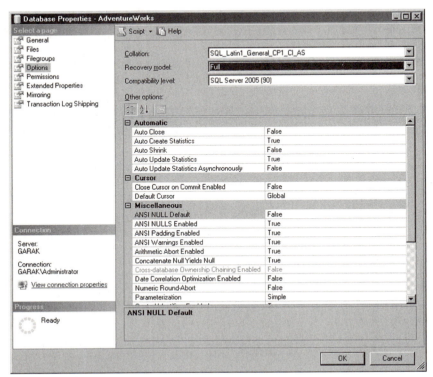

Figure 11-2
Database Properties—Options

4. Click **OK** to apply the changes.

5. Right click **AdventureWorks** under Databases, point to **Tasks**, and click **Back Up**.

6. In the Back Up dialog box, make sure AdventureWorks is the selected database to back up and the Backup type is Full (Figure 11-3).

7. Leave the default name in the Name box. In the Description box, type **Full Backup of AdventureWorks**.

8. Under Destination, a disk device may already be listed. If so, select the device, and click **Remove**.

9. Under Destination, click **Add**.

10. In the Select Back Up Destination box, click **Backup Device**, select **AdvWorksFull**, and click **OK**.

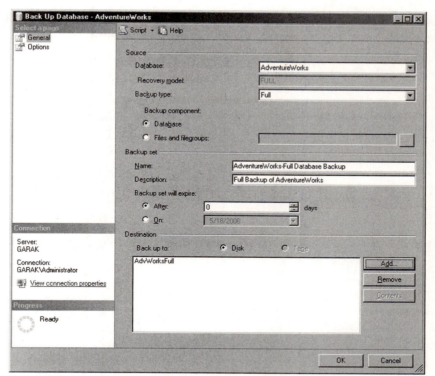

Figure 11-3
Backup Database Dialog Box—General Selection

11. You should now have a backup device listed under Destination. Switch to the **Options** page.

12. On the Options page (Figure 11-4), select **Overwrite all existing backup sets**. This option initializes a brand-new device or overwrites an existing one.

13. Select **Verify backup when finished** to check the actual database against the backup copy to be sure they match after the backup is complete.

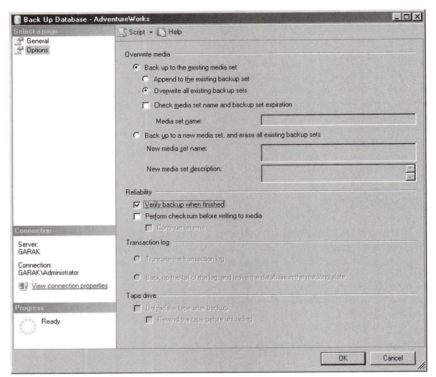

Figure 11-4
Backup Database Dialog Box—Options Selection

14. Click **OK** to start the backup.

15. Once completed, you have a full backup of the AdventureWorks database.

16. Take a moment to confirm that the backup is actually there. In Management Studio, expand Backup Devices under Server Objects in Object Explorer.

17. Right click **AdvWorksFull**, and select **Properties**.

18. On the Media Contents page (Figure 11-5), you should see the full backup of AdventureWorks.

19. Click **OK** to get back to Management Studio.

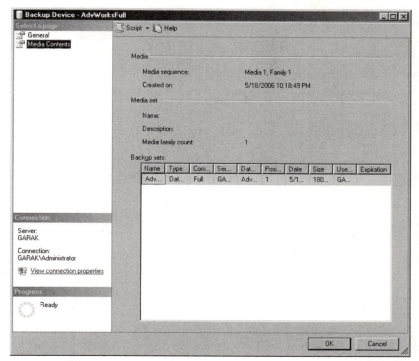

Figure 11-5
Backup Device Dialog Box—Media Contents Selection

■ PART B: Verifying Success

1. Return to Management Studio and instead of backups choose Restore from the context menu.
2. Your backup should be listed in the lower half of the dialog box.

Exercise 11.3	Backing Up a Database Using T-SQL Commands
Scenario	You want to automate the backup process using a SQL Server job. You can use the Maintenance Plan or create your own job using T-SQL code.
Duration	This task should take approximately 15 minutes.
Setup	For this task, you need access to a machine on which SQL Server is installed.
Caveat	You must have administrative privileges on SQL Server.
Procedure	In this task, you will work in the Query Editor.
Equipment Used	For this task, you need access to a machine on which SQL Server is installed.
Objective	To work with the Query Editor to manually perform a backup.
Criteria for Completion	This task is complete when the restore utility locates and displays your backup.

■ PART A: Backing Up a Database Using T-SQL Commands

1. Create a new backup device as you did in Exercise 11.1, but name it **master_backup**.
2. Open a Query Editor session by clicking **New Query** on the menu.
3. Enter the following command:

```
BACKUP DATABASE master TO master_backup WITH init;
```

4. The results should look something like Figure 11-6.

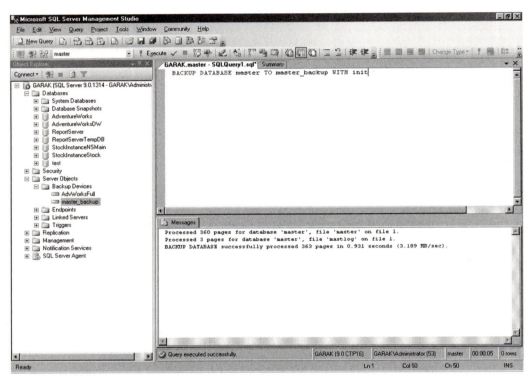

Figure 11-6
Management Studio Showing Backup Script

■ PART B: Verifying Success

1. Return to Management Studio and instead of Backup choose Restore from the context menu.
2. You should now have your backups listed in the lower half of the dialog box.

Exercise 11.4	Performing a Transaction Log Backup
Scenario	Your electric utility warned yesterday of potential and unpredictable blackouts in your area. You've learned you can restore to a point in time or just prior to the start of a stored procedure if you first perform a transaction log backup. You decide to schedule transaction log backups every ten minutes for the rest of the week. You also warn users to save their data entry records because they may have to check after any restore and reenter their last few transactions.
Duration	This task should take approximately 15 minutes.
Setup	For this task, you need access to a machine on which SQL Server is installed.
Caveat	You must have administrative privileges on Windows Server.
Procedure	In this task, you will work with Management Studio.
Equipment Used	For this task, you need access to a machine on which SQL Server is installed.
Objective	To work with Management Studio to create a transaction log backup.
Criteria for Completion	This task is complete when you have familiarized yourself with transaction log backups.

■ PART A: Performing a Transaction Log Backup

1. Open **Management Studio**. Expand your server and then expand the **Databases** node.
2. Right click **AdventureWorks**, point to **Tasks**, and select **Back Up**.
3. In the Back Up dialog box, make sure AdventureWorks is the selected database to back up and the Backup Type is Transaction Log.
4. Leave the default name in the Name box. In the Description box, type **Transaction Log Backup of AdventureWorks**.

5. Under Destination, make sure the AdvWorksFull device is listed (Figure 11-7).

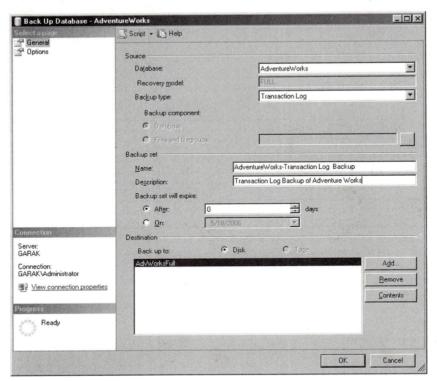

Figure 11-7
Backup Database—Transaction Log Type Backup

6. On the Options page, make sure **Append to the existing backup set** is selected so that you don't overwrite your existing full backup.

7. On the Options page, select **Verify backup when finished**.

8. Click **OK** to start the backup.

9. You should manually verify that the backup was completed. In Management Studio, expand **Backup Devices** under **Management** in **Object Explorer**.

10. Right click **AdvWorksFull**, and select **Properties**.

11. On the Media Contents page, you should see the transaction log backup of AdventureWorks.

12. Click **OK** to get back to Management Studio.

Exercise 11.5	Disabling a Database
Scenario	You're ready to restore a database. But first, make the AdventureWorks database suspect so that you can see exactly what SQL Server does to restore it. Specifically, blow away AdventureWorks.
Duration	This task should take approximately 15 minutes.
Setup	For this task, you need access to a machine on which SQL Server is installed.
Caveat	You must have administrative privileges on SQL Server.
Procedure	In this task, you will use operating system tools.
Equipment Used	For this task, you need access to a machine on which SQL Server is installed.
Objective	To deliberately destroy a database.
Criteria for Completion	This task is complete when Management Studio no longer displays AdventureWorks.

■ PART A: Disabling a Database

1. Right click **My Computer**, and select **Manage** from the context menu.
2. Expand **Services**, and select **SQL Server** for the instance to which you are currrently connected.
3. Right click **SQL Server** in the right pane, and click **Stop**. You'll be asked whether you wish to stop the SQLServerAgent service as well; click **Yes**.

> **NOTE**
>
> *You had to stop all SQL Server services because while they're running, all the databases are considered open files—you wouldn't be able to work with them outside of SQL Server.*

4. Find the file AdventureWorks_Data.mdf (usually in C:\Program Files\Microsoft SQL Server\MSSQL.1\MSSQL\Data\). This could be a different path if you are connected to a different instance.
5. Rename the file as **AdventureWorks_Data.old**.
6. Find the file AdventureWorks_Log.ldf, and rename it as **AdventureWorks_Log.old**.
7. From Computer Manager, restart the **SQL Agent** and **SQL Server** services.

■ PART B: Verifying Success

1. Open **Management Studio**, and expand **Databases** under your server name (Figure 11-8). Verify the absence of AdventureWorks.

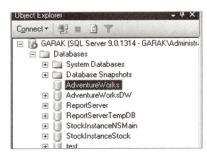

Figure 11-8
A Portion of Management Studio—Checking a Database

Question 1	*You could have detached the database to make it "disappear." Compare and contrast the two techniques. What does this method and the detach method do differently?*

Exercise 11.6	Performing a Simple Restore
Scenario	The disaster you prepared for has happened. Now that your database is gone, you need to restore it.
Duration	This task should take approximately 15 minutes.
Setup	For this task, you need access to a machine on which SQL Server is installed.
Caveat	You must have administrative privileges on SQL Server.
Procedure	In this task, you will work with Management Studio.
Equipment Used	For this task, you need access to a machine on which SQL Server is installed.
Objective	To restore a corrupt database.
Criteria for Completion	This task is complete when Management Studio displays AdventureWorks again.

■ PART A: Performing a Simple Restore

1. Right click **Databases**, and select **Restore Database**.
2. In the Restore Database dialog box, select **AdventureWorks** from the **To database** drop-down list box (Figure 11-9).

3. Under Source for restore, select **From device**. Click the ellipsis button (**...**) next to the text box to select a device.

4. In the Specify Backup dialog box, select **Backup Device** from the **Backup Media** drop-down list box, and click **Add**.

5. In the Select Backup Device dialog box, select **AdvWorksFull** and click **OK**.

6. Click **OK** to close the Specify Backup dialog box.

7. Under Select the backup sets to restore, select both backups (**Full** and **Transaction Log**). Doing so brings the database back to the most recent state. If you're in your production environment, you would also select any differential backups, log backups, and the tail log.

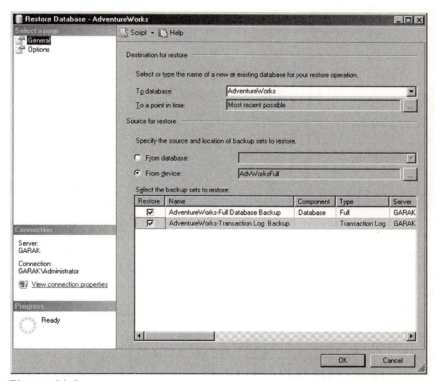

Figure 11-9
Restore Database—General Selection

8. On the Options page (Figure 11-10), make sure the **Restore With Recovery** option is selected under Recovery state, because you have no more backups to restore.

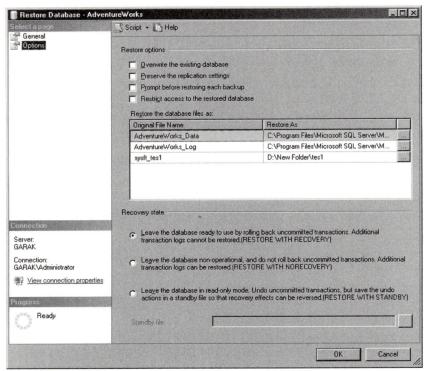

Figure 11-10
Restore Database—Options Selection

9. Click **OK** to begin the restore process.
10. In Management Studio, right click **Databases**, and click **Refresh**.

■ PART B: Verifying Success

1. Open **Management Studio**, and expand **Databases** under your server name. Verify the inclusion of AdventureWorks.

Exercise 11.7	Developing a Disaster Recovery Decision Tree
Scenario	You've just started work as the lead database administrator for the Yanni HealthCare Services Organization. Your first task is to update the existing database disaster recovery plan. You notice that the current plan doesn't address the issue of how to recover the LabOrders database when it has been marked as suspect. Your new disaster plan should cover this eventuality.
	The Yanni HealthCare database server is a two-node cluster with a single clustered SQL Server Enterprise Edition instance. The name of the virtual SQL Server cluster is YHC01. The cluster stores the quorum drive and all SQL

	Server databases on a shared disk on a Storage Area Network (SAN) device.
	Yanni HealthCare uses the following backup strategy for the LabOrders database:
	• A full database backup is made every second day at 18:00 with checksum validation.
	• A differential database backup is made on the intervening days at 18:00 with checksum validation
	• Transaction log backups are made every 20 minutes with checksum validation.
	The backup strategy is tested regularly and backup files are verified by using the checksum validation.
Duration	This task should take approximately 15 minutes.
Setup	A computer isn't required.
Caveat	There are no special requirements.
Procedure	This is a planning exercise.
Equipment Used	You might need paper and pencil.
Objective	To understand the choices and decisions involved with planning for a potential database recovery task.
Criteria for Completion	This task is complete when you have thought through and resolved a potential disaster.

■ PART A: Developing a Disaster Recovery Decision Tree

Do the following:
1. Devise a recovery strategy for the proposed scenario.
2. Define recovery success criteria.
3. Create a simple decision tree for what to do if the LabOrders database is marked as suspect.

NOTE	*Follow the paragraph headings in the "Developing a Database Disaster Recovery Plan" in your textbook to create a document.*

LAB 12
DESIGNING A DATA ARCHIVING SOLUTION

THIS LAB CONTAINS THE FOLLOWING EXERCISES AND ACTIVITIES:

Exercise 12.1   Applying the Strategy

Exercise 12.1	Applying the Strategy
Scenario	The Yanni HealthCare Network serves a total current population of 500,000 patients. During its 30-year history, it has registered approximately two million people for whom it has provided care. Currently, all medical laboratory diagnostic test results have been digitized and are maintained online in an On-Line Transaction Processing (OLTP) database. The laboratory results database has been growing at a rate of 1.5% per month and contains a large amount of data that is almost never updated and rarely queried. This obsolete data has slowed server-maintenance operations such as reindexing and defragmentation. Because of the large size of the database, running queries is becoming difficult. The final straw was reached when the chief of medicine requested a simple cross-tab query on three years' worth of data: The query began on a Friday and wasn't completed until Tuesday morning because of the sheer volume of records.
	Governmental health regulations require that all laboratory test results be maintained for 25 years. Clinical caregivers state that they require immediate access to the past five years' worth of data for queries and reports. Archived data must be available by the next day following the submission of the request. All data, as is the case with any medical data, must be secure and confidentiality maintained. There must be two copies of the archived data stored in different locales. In addition, risk-management personnel, accountants, and the research staff are insistent that all information be both retained online and archived. Finally, the organization has sufficient budget to purchase one or more new servers for storing the archived data.

Duration	This task should take approximately 30 minutes.
Setup	A computer isn't required.
Caveat	There are no special requirements.
Procedure	This is a planning exercise.
Equipment Used	You might need paper and pencil.
Objective	To compare your perspective with another person's—there is no one right answer.
Criteria for Completion	Stop when you feel comfortable with all the new concepts.

■ PART A: Applying the Strategy

Review these three questions, and answer them on your own before referring to the explanation that follows. If you disagree with the recommended solution, explain why.

1. Is replication appropriate to the archiving solution? Why or why not?

2. Design a replication topology. Identify the publisher, distributor, and subscriber. Specify the direction of replication.

3. Determine which type of replication to use and where. Defend your solution.

Possible Recommendations/Explanations

You need to determine whether you should recommend using replication with the archival data and when. As you'll recollect, there is a production database with the last 3 years of data, a database with data from the past 3 to 5 years, another archival database with data that is 6 to 25 years old, and a final archival database that contains data less than 25 years old.

The laboratory data is rarely updated after entry into the database and is only queried; hence, data conflicts aren't likely to arise. Data sent to the archival databases is marked read only. There is a regulatory requirement that a second copy must exist for all data less than 25 years old and must exist in a different location. The regulation also requires that data be secure.

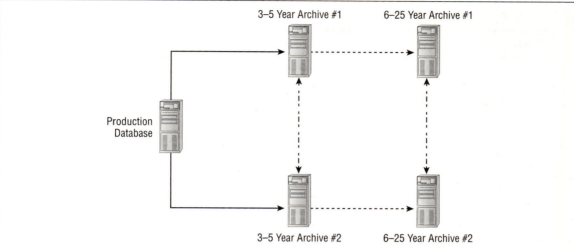

Figure 12-1
Possible points of replication are (1) between the production database and the 3–5 year archives, (2) between the 3–5 year archives and the 6–25 year archives, and (3) between each archive type.

Replication can be used with the archival data in this scenario in three possible places: between the production database and the first archival database, between the short-term archival database servers and the long-term archival database, and between the two copies of each database, as shown in Figure 12-1.

Replication between the production server and a short-term archival server isn't necessarily the only solution, but it can be used to update the data contained there on a regular basis. If you decide that replication fits your needs, the optimal solution is to implement transactional replication with the production database configured as the publisher and the short-term archival database server configured as a subscriber.

Replication between the two copies of the archival servers should also be configured as transactional replication. Transactional replication is the optimal choice:

- The structure of the data on the servers is the same, so data transformation isn't required.
- Data will be delivered with very low latency.

Merge replication isn't the best choice here because it has a higher latency than transactional replication. Multisite updates aren't required because data isn't modified once they're placed on the archival server.

Although it isn't ideal, snapshot replication should not be ruled out. As you saw earlier, snapshot replication is useful in circumstances where servers only need a read-only copy of the data and don't require updates very often.

However, you may reject a snapshot-replication solution because unlike transactional replication, which copies only data changes to subscribers, snapshot replication copies entire publications to subscribers every time it replicates. In this instance, you would overwrite the entire very large database each time you replicated between servers.

LAB SETUP GUIDE FOR DATABASE SERVER INFRASTRUCTURE DESIGN (70-443)

The *Microsoft SQL Server Database Design and Optimization* package of the Microsoft Official Academic Course (MOAC) series includes two books: a textbook and a lab manual. The exercises in the lab manual are designed for classroom use under the supervision of an instructor or a teaching assistant. In an academic setting, a computer classroom is commonly used by a variety of classes each day, so you must plan your setup procedure accordingly. For example, you might consider automating the classroom setup procedure and using removable fixed disks in the classroom and then removing the fixed disks after class each day.

The classroom labs and the textbook exercises use the Microsoft Windows default double-click setting: double-click to open an item (single-click to select) Do not configure the computers to use the optional setting (single-click to open an item; point to select).

COMPUTER HARDWARE AND SOFTWARE REQUIREMENTS

All hardware must be listed in the Windows Server Catalog. Here are the minimum requirements:

Table A-1
Windows Server 2008 Minimum requirements

Component	Requirement
Processor	Minimum: 1 GHz (x86 processor) or 1.4 GHz (x64 processor)
Memory	Maximum (32-bit systems): 4 GB (Standard) or 64 GB (Enterprise and Datacenter)
	Maximum (64-bit systems): 8 GB (Foundation) or 32 GB (Standard) or 2 TB (Enterprise, Datacenter, and Itanium-Based Systems)
	Minimum: 512 MB RAM

Disk space requirements	Minimum (32-bit systems): 20 GB or greater
	Minimum (64-bit systems): 32 GB or greater
	Foundation: 10 GB or greater
Display	Super VGA (800 × 600) or higher resolution monitor
Human interface device	Keyboard and Microsoft Mouse or compatible pointing device
Network interface device	Network interface card (NIC)
Bulk loading	DVD ROM drive

NOTE	*An Intel Itanium 2 processor is required for Windows Server 2008 for Itanium-Based Systems.*

NOTE	*Computers with more than 16 GB of RAM will require more disk space for paging, hibernation, and dump files. For this reason, consider disabling hibernation and memory dumps.*

NOTE	*Actual requirements will vary based on your system configuration, and the applications and features you choose to install. Processor performance is dependent upon not only the clock frequency of the processor, but the number of cores and the size of the processor cache. Disk space requirements for the system partition are approximate. Itanium-based and x64-based operating systems will vary from these disk size estimates. Additional available hard disk space may be required if you are installing over a network.*

Table A-2
Windows Server 2003 Minimum Requirements

Component	Requirement
Processor	Minimum: 550 GHz (x86 processor) or 733 GHz (x64 processor)
Memory	Maximum (32-bit systems): 4 GB (Standard) or 64 GB (Enterprise and Datacenter)
	Maximum (64-bit systems): 8 GB (Foundation) or 32 GB (Standard) or 2 TB (Enterprise, Datacenter, and Itanium-Based Systems)
	Minimum: 256 MB RAM (32-bit systems); 1 GB RAM (64-bit systems)

Disk space requirements	Minimum (32-bit systems): 20 GB or greater
	Minimum (64-bit systems): 32 GB or greater
	Foundation: 10 GB or greater
Display	Super VGA (800 × 600) or higher resolution monitor
Human interface	Keyboard and Microsoft Mouse or compatible pointing device
Network interface	Network interface card (NIC)
Bulk loading	CD ROM drive

NOTE	*A hard disk partition or volume with enough free space to accommodate the setup process. To ensure that you have flexibility in your later use of the operating system, we recommend that you allow considerably more space than the minimum required for running Setup, which is approximately 2 GB to 3 GB for x86-based versions of Windows Server 2003, and 4 GB for Itanium-based and x64-based versions of Windows Server 2003. The larger amount of space is required if you are running Setup across a network instead of from a CD-ROM, or if you are installing on a FAT or FAT32 partition in the case of x86-based or x64-based versions of Windows Server 2003. (NTFS is the recommended file system for both x86-based and x64-based versions of Windows Server 2003. Itanium-based versions of Windows Server 2003 support only NTFS).*

NOTE	*Using minimum requirements causes students to spend more time waiting that being constructive. Have a much better experience by using a CPU four times the minimum, RAM at two to four times the minimum, a hard disk at twice the minimum, a DVD ROM drive, and a flat screen monitor capable of a 1280 x 1024 pixel display (two monitors per student can be helpful).*

CLASSROOM SETUP FOR ALL COMPUTERS

- This course should be taught in a classroom containing networked computers that students can use for hands-on experience.
- Provide a standalone (workgroup-configured) Windows Server 2003 or Windows Server 2008 (need not be R2) clean install to every student with VisualStudio 2005 or VisualStudio 2008 preloaded and all service packs for both on a single partition of 20 or more gibibytes.

- The classroom setup described here assumes that you have a Dynamic Host Configuration Protocol (DHCP) server to provide IP addresses during system boot.
- Consider preloading SQL Server 2005 or SQL Server 2008 as learning to install the database system was covered in the prerequisite course *Microsoft SQL Server 2005 Implementation and Maintenance (70-431)*. Otherwise, the instructor could guide the students in loading SQL Server as a classroom and laboratory exercise using the guidance provided in the first book of this series. If so, everyone needs a loadable copy of SQL Server (preferably Enterprise Edition) available either as DVDs (or CDs) or on an available network share.
- The distribution DVD comes as a two DVD set and automatically prompts for the second DVD; the network share technique requires the manual starting of Disk 2. The instructor needs a heads up if this is the distribution method.

CLASSROOM SETUP FOR THE INSTRUCTOR'S COMPUTER

- The instructor needs the student configuration with the addition of PowerPoint, audio, current media player updates, and a working overhead projector. The instructor also needs to know the computer naming scheme, the student identification logon and the chosen classroom password (preferably Pa$$w0rd)

SETUP NOTES

- VisualStudio sometimes fails to load the first service pack on machines with less that a 1 GB of system memory (memory left over after the integrated video card takes its share)
- Do NOT use Virtual PC without at least 3 GBs of system memory (one for the operating system and two for SQL Server).
- Do NOT provide SQL Server on Vista; here's why: http://msdn2.microsoft.com/en-us/library/aa905868.aspx.
- Dual booting is fine.
- At some point, the operating system will ask each user to activate the server. When that happens, follow the steps to activate the product.

Notes

Notes

Notes

Notes